PSALLITE

Devotions and Prayers
for Church Choir Singers

Based on the Gospels, Series C, from
The Church Year Calendar and Lectionary

By Richard W. Patt

Publishing House
St. Louis

Concordia Publishing House, St. Louis, Missouri
Copyright © 1976 Concordia Publishing House

MANUFACTURED IN THE UNITED STATES OF AMERICA

Library of Congress Cataloging in Publication Data

Patt, Richard W
    Psallite.

    1. Choirs (Music)—Prayer books and devotions—
English. I. Title.
BV4596.C48P37   242'.6'9   76-47672
ISBN 0-570-03748-4

Author's Preface

These devotions and prayers are offered to individual church choir members and directors as their own personal devotions, thereby giving them an opportunity to worship the Lord for whom they sing. The book contains a devotion for every week of the church year, plus several major festivals. It is suggested that the members be encouraged to use this devotional material each week prior to the worship service.

These devotions and prayers may also be shared collectively at the beginning of the weekly choir rehearsal. To distinguish the three sections of material in each devotion, two choir members may be assigned to serve as readers. One announces and reads the Scripture passage, the other reads the devotion, and the first concludes the devotion with the prayer. The prayer to be used before the worship service may also be used as a collective prayer by the entire choir, spoken by all or by an appointed leader.

Since this devotional material is based on the Gospels for each Sunday beginning with The First Sunday in Advent (Series C of *The Church Year Calendar and Lectionary*, a three-year system of readings), the users of this devotional material will have an opportunity to prepare for Sunday and other special worship services by automatically becoming acquainted with the Gospel reading for these services. Prayers are also included for Monday, Tuesday, and Wednesday of Holy Week.

These devotions will not only be an opportunity for choir members to worship but will get the weekly rehearsal off to a good start, instilling the singers with the purpose for which they have come together, namely, to use their time and talents in serving the Lord through music.

Richard W. Patt
Milwaukee, Wisconsin
The Epiphany of our Lord, 1976

To all the choirs
of Sherman Park Lutheran Church, Milwaukee,
and their director of music, Mr. Scott Riedel,
carrying on more than a grand tradition—but that too

Festivals, Texts, Themes

The Season After Pentecost

Lesser Festivals and Commemorations

First Sunday in Advent   Luke 21:25-36

Are You Ready for This?

This Sunday brings the worshiping church to the beginning of
another Advent season. Most of us feel we're ready for it. For
week upon week now we have been counting the Sundays of
Pentecost. The lessons and liturgy of these weeks have been
good. But now we're ready for Advent! We're ready for this
happy season that brings us to the glory of Christmas

Or are we ready? Listening to this Sunday's Gospel, talking
as it does about signs in sun and moon and stars, about distress
of nations and people fainting, and the Son of Man coming in a
cloud with glory, one is moved to ask, are we ready for *this*?

Advent is a beautiful season, but also one that challenges us
to the claims of the coming Lord. Ours is no comfortable faith,
where Jesus merely cheers us on as we build a calm and collected
life for ourselves here on earth. He calls us to have a vision of
the end of all things, so that we serve Him faithfully and
urgently in the days we have here. Even this choir music must
be more than putting together sounds that please and soothe
us. Today we must make of this the *Lord's* music, as we give our
hearts to the Advent Savior!

Prayer: Lord Jesus Christ, we believe that You are coming again. So
we ask You to give all our songs an urgency that will help call people to
You and Your kingdom. We worship You for Your lowly coming
among us in Bethlehem. We praise You for Your present grace and
favor in our lives; and we humbly pray that You will keep us in faith
until we see Your coming again in clouds of glory. Amen.

Prayer before worship: Blessed Lord, our hearts are filled with Advent
excitement. We begin a new season of worship in Your name! Keep our
acts of praise fresh and vibrant for months to come, and use our songs
today to lift up the hearts of all people in praise of Your coming. Amen.

11

Preparing the Way of the Lord

There are few more familiar or beloved passages of church music than the opening strains of Handel's great oratorio, *Messiah*. Listen:

"The voice of one crying in the wilderness: prepare the way of the Lord, make His paths straight. Every valley shall be filled, and every mountain and hill shall be brought low, and the crooked shall be made straight, and the rough ways shall be made smooth; and all flesh shall see the salvation of God." Perhaps most of us know these words more as coming from the Advent section of the *Messiah* than their original source in Isaiah 40!

The theme, in any case, is "preparing the way of the Lord." Road building and repairs are pictured here as a necessary human activity.

Isn't it true that we sometimes don't appreciate road builders? They make the way temporarily bumpy. They force us to take detours. They raise dust and cause a general inconvenience.

But how necessary their work is! Smooth, level roadways result. Steep valleys and blunt upward grades are avoided. It has been worth the wait and inconvenience after all!

Our privilege and call as singers in worship during these holy Advent days is the same. We are preparing the way. We are announcing the coming of the Savior in our chants and hosannas and anthems. God calls us to be partners with Him in announcing the coming of His kingdom!

Our songs need to be especially firm and trumpet-like these Advent days. We are inviting our fellow worshipers to receive their King. Jesus comes in mercy and love!

Like all road builders, our work may not always be appreciated. When is the last time you received a compliment for singing the Lord's song? Maybe you can't remember. No matter. Our call is to sing with faith and with the love of Christ in our hearts. As a few heard the voice of Isaiah, and the words of Jesus, so some will hear us too—and Advent will happen again. Let us now be about our work of "preparing the way of the Lord."

Prayer: Lord, we are preparing Your way by singing a new song to You. We want our music to be a road leading straight to You. As we use our tools of breathing and rhythm and harmony, help us to make it easier for Your love and forgiveness and peace to reach the hearts of all this Sunday. Amen.

Prayer before worship: Heavenly Lord, in these exciting days before Christmas, when so much begins to be on our minds, give us grace to always welcome Your coming with highest delight. As we now enter Your house of prayer and worship, likewise enter our hearts and minds, opening our lips in joy to chant Your praise and glory. Give beauty to our song and life to the words we sing, that Christ may make His Advent among Your people today. In the name of Him whose way we prepare! Amen.

This Is Good News?

These words call for some explanation. After all, we are tempted to ask, "This is *good news?*"

John the Baptizer is talking about the coming of the Advent Lord, Jesus Christ. To get ready for this coming, he addresses his hearers as a brood of poisonous snakes, threatening that their tree will be laid low by a fierce ax if it isn't producing just right. And furthermore they will be asked to give up most of what they had knocked themselves out for, trying during a lifetime to attain it. When Jesus comes, there will be a clear-cut harvest, with wheat going to the granary and all chaff burned in never-ending fire. I say, we are ready to ask, "*This* is the good news of Advent?"

Well, yes, good news because it signals that the real Messiah is to be found in Jesus of Nazareth. For not only will the coming Advent Lord demand sacrifice of the people, but He Himself will live in radical servanthood and sacrifice, ready and willing to give up all so that God's will of rescue and salvation may be accomplished for all the earth.

The good news is that Jesus was finally baptized in the fires of death at the cross, suffering and going to the grave without flinching or failure, bringing us rescue and deliverance from a similar fate.

Good news indeed! Serving and suffering, Jesus is delivering us from eternal fires, lifting us to a life of purpose and joyful service now. This good news will make our songs and singing for Him full of gladness and happy expectation!

Prayer: Coming Savior, Advent Lord, thanks to You for enduring what we shun, for accepting what we despise, and for making good news out of what we may regard a bad deal. Open our lips to sing Your praise. Open our hearts to receive Your saving presence. Instill our singing here with an air of expectancy, and grant us all Your Advent joy. Amen.

Prayer before worship: Jesus, our Savior, we are coming to You with the rest of the congregation today, in humility and repentance. May the fruit of our repentance be faith in You, freed in forgiveness, ready to serve You in everything we say and do. Give us such godly intent as we now enter to praise You, the Spirit and our Father, one God forever. Amen.

True Christian Honor

It is an old Christian custom that we should always welcome the begging stranger who comes to our door. After all, the reasoning goes, you never know that the stranger might be Jesus Christ Himself! Any of us would indeed be honored to have Christ at our door, visiting in our home. Thus it is that Elizabeth properly honored Mary as the bearer of Christ when she asked, "And why is this granted me, that the mother of my Lord should come to me?" As if to say, "In my own sinful unworthiness, there is no reason why the Lord of heaven should come under my roof."

How true. How profound. What mystery of God indeed, that He should visit us! But this is at the very heart of the Christmas message, isn't it so? Christ *does* come, and He comes to our places where sin and human pride hold sway. He comes, and *we* become the beggars, pleading for the Bread of Life to feed us, for the Water of Life to quench our thirst. And He does!

What honor bestowed on us. Jesus Christ makes His glorious Advent, and we are saved. O happy day!

Prayer: Lord, it is always positively amazing the way You are willing to come to us wherever we are. Today we ask You to come among us here as we seek to offer songs of celebration at Your Christmas coming. Transform these moments now as we realize our high calling of making melody in praise and worship of Your Advent. Hear us as we pray in Your name. Amen.

Prayer before worship: Almighty Father, we stand in amazement at Your love. You are calling us to Your house. You are inviting us to Your table. You are bringing us to the glory and light of Christmas. May we all hear the good news in our worship now as we accept and celebrate anew Your love and grace in our lives. Through the Christ of Bethlehem we pray. Amen.

John 1:1-18

The Word Made Flesh

These are days of glory for every church choir! People want Christmas music in their worship. During these days worshipers seem especially receptive to our musical efforts. After all, what would Christmas—and Christmas church services—be without our glorious songs?

On the other hand, what would all our singing add up to these days without the glorious *fact* of Christmas: Jesus Christ was born in a stable; the Word was made flesh!

At Christmas we are rejoicing—and singing—about God's love and grace invading our lives, melting away the ice of pride and selfishness, the winter of man's sin and shame. The Light has shined. The Word was made flesh.

This gives our Christmas songs a special purpose. Our ringing voices, our blending of rhythm and harmony and all the other dynamics of choral production, linked as they are to the message of Jesus, can help make the Word flesh for others. That's the real glory of our musical task these days: that Christ be made more real, more in grasp, more in flesh for those who come seeking Him in the manger.

So sing, choirs of angels! Sing in exultation!

Prayer: Lord, we are thankful that we have a new song to sing this Christmas: the ever-new message of grace and hope and love in Your Son, Jesus Christ. Use our melody, with all the other bright things of Christmas, to exalt the Word made flesh, even Christ, our Lord. Amen.

Prayer before worship: O Christ of Bethlehem, O Son of Mary, we give You our hearts again on this glad day (night). With excitement and gratitude we welcome Your coming. Now listen to our songs, Lord Jesus, offered to You in thanks and praise for Your life, death, and rising. May Your Christmas peace be over us today and always! Amen.

A Living Hope

Did our Christmas music make any difference at all? The hours
of rehearsal, the extra time and concentration that we gave—
what did it all add up to?

Quite a bit, no doubt. At least we hope it did. We hope that
the glorious worship of these past days was a blessing for many,
that along with us a host of others were drawn closer to Christ.

Let us always thus hope and count on God's Holy Spirit to be
moving and working among us! The same Spirit once revealed
to Simeon of old that he should not give up hope for salvation
through the coming Christ. He and the prophetess Anna have
been outstanding examples of *a living hope* in a God who comes,
who does visit and save His people.

The living hope of Simeon was richly blessed as he held the
Babe in his arms, singing, "Mine eyes have seen Thy salvation!"

Does our singing make any difference, we wonder. Does our
life mean anything more because of Christmas? Oh, yes, it does.
The same Spirit who planted hope in the hearts of Simeon and
Anna has shined among us in the face of Jesus Christ. His grace
and mercy, and His power to save are coming to many hearts
during these Christmas days. Christ is our living Hope!

Prayer: Lord, as things begin to let up a little during these days after
Christmas, keep a living hope alive in us. Cheer us and lift up our
hearts even now with the presence and power of Jesus, our Savior. In
His holy name we pray. Amen.

Prayer before worship: O Christ Child, weak in the manger and lowly in
birth, help us in worship now to see the true glory of Your coming. As
we rejoice in Your lowliness, help us also to worship You in Your
suffering and death on the cross, that Your full glory may be seen and
believed by all. Hear our prayer, O Christ. Amen.

All Hail the Power of Jesus' Name

Our worship for the Name of Jesus falls on the first day of the new calendar year, January 1. It is obviously a happy coincidence that, as we begin a new year, the name of Jesus should be on our minds.

Whenever someone's dear name is on our minds, it seems we like to impress the fact somehow. Ninth-grade boys carve the name of their true love on homeroom desks. Over-zealous lovers imprint their joint initials on the trunks of lovely trees, while others deface concrete overpasses with the painted names of their latest sweetheart.

In this Christmas season we have learned a new name of love, and we can't help singing about it! "All hail the power of Jesus' name!"

What power indeed rests in the name of our beloved Savior! Though frail and tiny now in His bed of straw, He will grow to manhood and be baptized as the suffering Servant and Savior of the world. Even now, He lies in the manger as King of kings and Lord of lords, dreaming of Easter victory.

Though now an infant meek and mild, we cannot help glorifying His name, for we know that by His death and rising we are saved.

Prayer: Lord, we are thankful that You lived up to Your name. Through death on the cross and victory over the grave on Easter, You have been lifted up as King of all. Keep us and guide us with Your saving hand in all the days of the new year to come. Amen.

Prayer before worship: Gracious Father, who shared Your Son with us in suffering and love, bless all Your gathered family now as we meet on this new year in the strong name of Jesus, Savior of all and Lord of nations. Amen.

A Christmas Hymn

The carols and hymns of Christmas have again proven their popularity. As a choir we have enjoyed singing them too.

But a Bible text like the one we have just read reminds us that the carols of Christmas dare never be mere mood music. Did you notice how many of the vibrant holy songs of yuletide became just that: background music to accompany the over-spending of department store customers? Even in the churches we have sometimes sought "Christmasy" music to fill in the gaps of our festival worship service.

This lofty passage that opens John's Gospel here is actually one of the earliest Christmas hymns in exaltation of the newborn Savior. But it is anything but "Christmasy" background music! It is a song with meaning and message. It is a text that puts us face to face with Him who created all things and then entered His creation as the merciful Child of Bethlehem.

That's our projected task in these coming weeks of Epiphany worship: to hold up Jesus Christ as the divine Son of God, as God of God and Light of Light. He will have no background place in the lives of people. He is no religious fill-in to create soothing moods when life gets challenging and rough.

He is the Word that begins all our words, and He is the last Word who will bring us to final glory. We will sing of this lofty Christ in the weeks to come! Let us be about our music-making with devotion and awe.

Prayer: Christ, You are the Word made flesh, the saving Word of the Father to us all. Grant that our gathering today may be a time of fellowship in faith and joy in sharing Your love with many. Hear our prayer and brighten this hour. Amen.

Prayer before worship: Father of mercies, and God of grace, give Your guidance and wisdom to all who lead us in worship. For pastors and musicians, for all who come to worship You here today, may this be a blessed and renewing hour. In Jesus' name we pray. Amen.

I'd Like to Teach the World to Sing

There is a song, popular among young people, that says, "I'd like to teach the world to sing." That is a fine goal for any Christian, it seems. After all, what the song writer is hoping for is not just that mankind becomes the world's largest mass choir. The hope is rather for peoples of all places and faces to dwell together in peace and love. This is the "harmony" of which the song dreams.

That's exactly God's dream for the world! That's the universal mission of our Epiphany Lord. Already as an infant the Babe begins to draw people of different places together. The Wise Men who sought Him were Gentile worshipers from the East. The dream was on the way.

Someone has observed that music is the international language understood by all. Christ is the Savior of the nations, for all can understand His mercy and love. The cross does not need explaining. It is the Father's act of love and rescue for all people everywhere. Today the cross embraces us with its saving power, and it seeks to enfold all people.

Part of our privilege as singers for the Lord is always this blessed mission enterprise of making Christ's all-embracing love more attractive and real for any who hear us.

"I'd like to teach the world to sing." Come along and declare now your mission in song!

Prayer: Jesus, You showed us that You are the Christ, Son of the living God. Your love is wide enough and broad enough for all the world. Thank You for including us in Your circle of love. Use our songs to widen that circle among us. Amen.

Prayer before worship: On this festival of light, O Jesus, shine brightly among us with Your mercy and love. Show Yourself as divine Lord, that all the world may come to worship You. Visit our minds and hearts with Your Spirit, that this festival may be a celebration of faith. In the name of the Father and Spirit, we pray to You, O Christ. Amen.

Look What Happened to the Baby!

It seems like only yesterday we were worshiping the Babe in the manger, the Christ of Christmas. But today, look what happened to the Baby!

Not only has the Child of Bethlehem grown up, but He has ceased being the meek and mild Babe we peered at just a while ago. Now He carries a winnowing fork in His hand. He is about to clear the threshing floor. The wheat will be gathered in, and the chaff will be burned. Look! He baptizes not with water, but with the Holy Spirit and fire. And in His own Baptism, the Spirit descends as a dove, and the Father's voice is heard from heaven. Oh, look what happened to the Baby!

This Baptism sets the Son on His mission. It presses Him on the path toward the cross. The Lord begins His saving work.

This Baptism surely reminds us of our own. Or does it? What has happened to the babes throughout history, baptized into the name of Jesus? Hopefully our lives have been changed and new goals set when we were marked with the sign of the cross.

Obedience to the Lord's will is now our delight, even as Christ in Baptism submitted to the Father's will. His presence and power in our life will help accomplish it!

Prayer: Lord Jesus Christ, You gave Yourself over completely to the Father's plan when You were baptized in Jordan's stream. Help us give ourselves completely now to Your service as we make songs of praise to Your name. Amen.

Prayer before worship: Blessed Savior, today we remember how You showed complete obedience to the Father, as You were baptized. Now may we use this worship hour to renew our baptism and to follow You in Your way more closely than ever. Give us this fruit of faith today, O Jesus. Amen.

Wine, Women, and Song

"Wine, women, and song" may seem like an irreverent theme for a devotional focus. It even gets facetious when we recall what one comic soul referred to as the poor man's version of it: "beer, the old lady, and television!" But surprisingly, Sunday's Gospel tells us that Jesus approved of all three! And for that we are grateful.

First, our Lord joined in a celebration that included the sensuous fruit of the vine. Jesus assured an abundant supply of wine. Second, he delights in a woman being joined in marriage to her chosen partner. Third, no doubt music filled the scene as well. Wine, women, and song: the elements of our everyday living and celebration—Jesus affirmed them here.

Likewise He affirms *our* song today as well. Know this, dear friend: Jesus Christ wants us to sing our songs. He wants us to be about our music-making in His name.

Because of Him we really do have a song to share. We have a salvation and new life to celebrate. As something new begins in every marriage, celebrated in wine and music, so we are new creations in Christ. His cross and rising have ushered in a new age of peace and hope for all of us. So we celebrate, and so we sing.

Prayer: Father in heaven, You give us many gifts each day in our lives. Because of them we have reason to praise You. Grant that we may rightly use all things, including our talents and time, so that Your name will be honored. We thank You especially for the gift of Your Son, whose love and mercy shined among us when He died on the cross and rose again. Help us now to offer a feast of song for You, that it may give honor and glory to Your Son, our Savior, Jesus Christ. Amen.

Prayer before worship: Lord, all things are joining together in this hour to praise Your name. The beauty of the sanctuary, stone, and glass of many colors; vestments and cloth in rich array; words of liturgy, carefully and solemnly written; message of pulpit; bread for breaking, wine for pouring; music and song to fill the space of Your house. Take all of these offerings and fill them with Your Spirit, that our worship may spring from our hearts and our song may take wings. In the praise of Jesus hear us. Amen.

The Spirit of the Lord upon Us!

We're not that far into a new year. How shall we manage all the weeks and months to come? This Sunday's Gospel gives us some unambiguous clues in answer.

Look at the life of Jesus! In these verses we see Him beginning His public ministry. It was the most fruitful ministry of all God's sons. How did He do it?

The opening word here gives us direction. *"Jesus returned in the power of the Spirit."* Our Lord Himself points His observers to a word of Isaiah, "The Spirit of the Lord is upon Me," He reads, applying the sacred text to Himself.

Herein lies the answer, and the sacred secret, to the amazingly fruitful ministry of the Son of God. The power of the Spirit was in Him, and the Spirit of the Lord rested on Him. All of which is to say that Jesus allowed God and His will to work in Him fully.

And that is the key for us in the months to come! We shall manage each day very well "in the power of the Spirit." Even our singing and music for the Lord will come to new success when we are fully open to God's Spirit and His prompting.

Now, how to be filled with this Spirit? Look to Jesus! See Him as Epiphany Lord, as Suffering Servant, as Easter King. He has rescued us and saved us. Now our hearts are open to receive the power of the Spirit.

Prayer: Christ, we praise You for showing us the power of the Spirit in Your life and ministry. Now send us the same Spirit as we remember Your life—and death—for us. Unite our voices now, and our hearts, that in our music here Your name will be praised. Hear our prayer, Lord Jesus. Amen.

Prayer before worship: Father in heaven, this is the hour of the Spirit's coming. In Word and Sacrament His power is dispensed among us. Grant that His coming now may show us the face of Your merciful Son, so that truly believing in Him, our songs may be filled with new life and worship that is true. In Jesus' name we pray. Amen.

This Is It!

The Christmas season so quickly past has a smoothness and lilt about it that tends to take the edge off its jolting reality. The Word made flesh! God dwells among the people! The sweet Babe of the manger has now grown to manhood, and behold, we are face to face with the Godhead. This is it! In Jesus Christ we are face to face with the Lord Himself.

This encounter, we know, is in dead earnest. It is filled with confrontation and challenge. So the folks of Jesus' hometown found out when their familiar-face Boy-become-rabbi returned to Nazareth. Now He came not as their equal but as their Messiah. This is it!—they knew shortly after His opening words in the synagog. He who used to make His home among us comes to tell us that now *God* would make His home among us— claiming us, calling us, using us as His people to do His work in the world.

No God at a safe distance anymore. He is now among us and we must decide. This is it!

The folks in Nazareth-town became angry and rose up to put their Lord out of the city. Leading Him to the brow of the hill at city's edge, they were ready to jump the gun on His own crucifixion. They were not up to His challenging call.

Neither are we, when self and comforts and security and peace are the only premiums we seek after. Even our songs, then, hard as we try, will sound flat. And what is worse than flat singing?

This is it! Christ wants more than our musically prepared song today. He wants our will and our heart and ourselves. So He stands before us, and so we say, "Here I am, Lord."

Prayer: O Lord, how shall we meet Thee? How do we stand up to Your glorious revelation and Epiphany? Not in our own strength or wisdom, to be sure. But in seeing Your lordship and leading, we know we can follow wherever You take us to do Your will and be Your people. Make our songs signs and sounds of our discipleship as we follow You! Amen.

Prayer before worship: O God, the hour of encounter is here again. The time of meeting You is upon us. Praise to You for this time of grace and favor. Lift up our hearts in song and word and action, that all may come to know who Your Son is: Jesus Christ, Lord and Savior of all. In His name we say, Amen.

Get Ready for the Unexpected

Choir rehearsals can get to be very much like fishing excursions. After a while you know just what to expect.

And that is not all bad. Reality tells us that much of our life will be like that. There are jobs to get done and assignments to fulfill. It was especially true in the starkly non-technological surroundings of ancient Palestine.

But even with our wide-ranging activities today, brought on by scientific wizardry, we are essentially in the same boat. The daily task needs doing. The ordinary demands remain ordinary. The fishermen needed a catch, and so they launched out as they had done hundreds of times before. We want to sing on Sunday mornings, so we rehearse. We know just about what to expect.

But for those early disciples mentioned in Luke 5 Jesus and His presence made a difference. The work was carried out in all its technical aspects just like it had always been. But now there was a great catch of fish. Jesus made it so!

So now, get ready for the unexpected. *Jesus is present among us too.* We meet as people of faith. We have all seen the glory of the light shining in a manger. We have beheld the Word, and we have called Him our Lord as the Holy Spirit has prompted us. This ordinary work we do is done in the presence of Christ.

So we look for the vitality He always brings to the scene. We look for special insights into the sacred words and musical notes. We view each other as fellow singers in the Lord's service. We see our director as the Lord's servant and our call to sing as an unexpected honor bestowed by Christ Himself.

Prayer: Blessed Savior, You brought unexpected joys to Your disciples of old. Your gracious presence always made the difference. So come, Lord Jesus, abide with us and make ours truly "a new song." We pray in Your name. Amen.

Prayer before worship: Lord, as Your disciples let down the net and unfolded a great catch, so we now bring our empty hearts before You in sacrifice and praise. Fill them with Your presence and give us the new life of Your Spirit that our worship may truly be alive. Hear us, O Lord. Amen.

Yes or No?

Sometimes we observe human situtations that are so tragic as to be almost comical. The drunken person in his stupor is a sad case, yet his actions and talk may carry a note of comedy. Some people are so utterly poverty-stricken that only a sense of humor about it carries them through each day.

When we hear these words of Jesus in this famous sermon, we don't know whether we should laugh or cry. Is he really serious, or is it all a put-on? After all, look what he says here! Poor people and hungry folks should be happy. Those who are being hated now should take it with a smile. And the rich people? Well, one day they won't be rich anymore.

Can we accept Jesus' words here? For the fact is that He is dead serious about them. So radical is His talk here that it is either altogether true or totally false. What do we say, yes or no? There can be no middle ground with words like these!

The words *are* to be accepted, of course. And they can be, for they were validated in the very actions of Jesus Himself. He was poor and hungry and now the kingdom of God is His. He allowed men to hate Him, even until it brought Him to the cross. But now He is lifted up in glory and reigns as Epiphany Lord. In Jesus' life we see that, once we say yes completely to God's will and way, He *does* lead us and keep us as our loving Father.

Today Christ stands before us. Are you with Me or against Me, He asks. By the aid of His gracious spirit may each of us answer, "Yes, Lord, here I am. I am Your servant."

Prayer: Lord Jesus, Your faithfulness to the Father's will has brought us salvation. When love even to death was needed, You went to the cross, and the Father brought You to Easter victory. Now we may sing and rejoice and confidently say yes to all Your words and invitations, for You will go with us and fulfill all things. Amen.

Prayer before worship: Now is the hour of worship. Now is the hour of song. Now is the hour of praising. Now is the hour of joy. Accept our heartfelt praises and give us courage and confidence for all that is to come. In Jesus' name. Amen.

Luke 9:28-36

A Glimpse of Divinity

Transfiguration is one of those happy festivals of the church. The theme of brightness and light are inherent in the day's observance.

A few disciples go up an ordinary hillside with their Lord. Soon all heaven breaks loose. In dazzling white the Savior stands glorified. Jesus gives the three surprised beholders a glimpse of divinity.

The same can be true of our songs. They might just give some of our fellow worshipers a taste of heaven and a glimpse of the divine.

"*Our* choir, *these* voices?" Well yes, who knows what glorious thoughts and visions are released in the minds of those who share our singing faith?

We sing of a loving Savior, of a fired Spirit, and a merciful Father of grace. All the possibilities are there for heaven itself to be opened.

How important our songs are! What mission we are performing when the message of Christ is carried by our voices and music!

In the death and rising of Jesus we have caught a glimpse of divinity: God loving you and me and bringing us eternal rescue. And our singing can give others the same glimpse of a merciful Lord!

Prayer: Lord, we confess that often our hearts and lives are darker than need be because we are not seeking the light in You. In Your Son the true light has shined forth. He has given us a glimpse of Your loving and forgiving face. We thank You for the mission of Your Son, and we ask You to so lighten our hearts that others may catch a glimpse of Your presence in us. Give us concentration, dedication, and godly zeal now as we sing Your message. In the name of Jesus. Amen.

Prayer before worship: Lord, You have the power to change anything. Where there is darkness, You can bring light. Where there is despair, You can bring hope. Where we can see only things human, You can give us a glimpse of the divine. Bring Your changing power to our time of worship now, so that all may see and worship the Sun of Righteousness—Jesus Christ the Lord. Amen.

The Secret Life of Faith

In these words Jesus is not saying that we should practice our religion in private only. Otherwise we would not have to be singing our songs for Ash Wednesday worship! What Jesus says, He says very clearly: "Beware of practicing your piety before men *in order to be seen by them.*" We may practice our religion before people—as long as the motives are right.

That's what's so good about *first* carrying out the sacred rites of our faith *in private.* That's what's good about the discipline of Lent. Both control us to make our religion authentic within first of all. Then it will no doubt be authentic, and acceptable to the Father, when practiced in public.

The season of Lent and the solemn day of Ash Wednesday pose a risk for worshiping Christians. They will either be days when the shallowness of our faith is confirmed in even more irrelevant outward acts. Or they will be days when a glorious inward faith, wrought in us by the Holy Spirit, shines forth in beautiful outward acts of prayer and offering and self-denial. Why will we celebrate Lent? What will our motives be? Let us trust the Holy Spirit to lead the way!

Prayer: O Christ, we know we can do no good thing without You. We know You have done all good things for us. Now we desire to offer You the special worship of another season of Lent. Enlarge our faith, correct our motives, and give us all the grace to humbly worship at the foot of Your cross. Amen.

Prayer before worship: Once again, O Lord, we come to the season of the cross. We are privileged to receive its forgiveness and share its message. It all points us to Your divine love, Lord Jesus. May our music today reflect the deep praise and profound thanks within us. In Your name of love we pray, our Savior. Amen.

The High Call of Lent

Sometimes we get things all switched around. What is unimportant we regard as supremely important. What really matters we are quick to discard.

The high call of Lent is to get our priorities in order, so that God might be glorified and served in all of our life.

Jesus had to do that. In the Bible text we see Him in the wilderness, being tempted by Satan. Jesus was there in the first place no doubt because He knew the proper priorities. He was preparing for a great task—the divine work of man's salvation. He would have to suffer and die for the people! To keep His eye on *that* kind of priority would mean having all the lesser priorities in order too.

Satan tempted Him precisely at these crucial points, but He remained faithful to the larger priority—the Word of God and the Father's will. That is our high calling in Lent—to see the Word as all important! Can it be? More important than my career and its development? More important than purchasing power for the sake of my family's comfort? More important than flashy church programs that pack the pews?

Lent calls us to focus on and trust God's Word. His promises will bring us all we are really looking for. Christ was crucified, and died—and the third day there was *victory*. Let us use this beautiful, solemn season of Lent to confirm and keep firm our determination to make God's Word and way the center of our lives and work!

Prayer: Jesus our Lord, the sacred season of Lent is upon us. You are the center of it all. You kept us and our deep spiritual need in mind, and so You went to the cross for us! Thank You, Jesus, for remaining faithful in our behalf. Now help *us* to accept the high call of Lent—to trust Your Word and do Your will. Amen.

Prayer before worship: Lord Jesus Christ, amid these days of Lent our lips cannot keep silence. We must praise You in grateful song. Make our chief priority now the Word You have to share with us in preaching and sacrament. May all hearts be focused there, so Your Holy Spirit will enter our lives and show us Your way. In Your name we say, Amen.

God's Yearning Heart

Sometimes good goals in our life become too much for us. Life overwhelms us, and we give in to lesser dreams than we might have.

But not even physical danger could keep Jesus from His appointed task—our eternal salvation and hope in this life. Herod was out to kill Him. And if not Herod now, then one day the Pharisees and people would.

In the face of mounting physical threats, Jesus was determined to finish His course. Why so? Because as the Son of God He had *a yearning heart*. More than anything He wanted people to be open to God's liberating and healing love. He wanted them to know of His Father's deep desire. So He exclaimed in frustration how all this good news had been laid before Jerusalem but had been spurned nevertheless.

But Jesus never gave up seeking our good, and so He allowed Himself to be given over to crucifixion and death. We praise Him during these days for that.

If sometimes our songs and their preparation seem tedious, relentless, or repetitive, let us recall our mission as the Lord's singers. We too are seeking and yearning to sing and thus share the good news of salvation in Jesus Christ. May this high mission keep us attentive and faithful to our work!

Prayer: Lord Jesus Christ, Your seeking heart has found us, and we are saved! May all our songs now be anthems of praise and adoration to Your holy name. Help us all to sing and share our message of Your love with dedication and prayer. Amen.

Prayer before worship: O blessed God, we have tried to worship You all week in our words and lives. Now we come to confess our failures and shortcomings. Renew us by Your grace and set us on the path again. Thus may this hour be bright with the promise and hope that only You can give it. In Jesus' name, we ask it. Amen.

A Second Chance

God is always giving us another chance, isn't He? Sometimes we can't wait to pronounce the verdict on others. We like to set limits, scold, and then lower the boom. Sometimes we bring people around by reminding them that this is their last chance.

But God, it seems, always hesitates to thus exclude us from His circle of love. He sees our lack of accomplishment for good. He notices our willful setting out on our own paths and goals. But He brings us back to Himself through His own unique brand of steadfast love. He is long-suffering. He has a patience that can only be labeled divine. He is always giving us a second chance. Listen to Jesus' parable: "A man had a fig tree planted in his vineyard; and he came seeking fruit on it and found none. And he said to the vinedresser, 'Lo, these three years I have come seeking fruit on this fig tree, and I find none. Cut it down; why should it use up the ground?' And he answered him, 'Let it alone, sir, this year also, till I dig about it and put on manure. And if it bears fruit next year, well and good; but if not, you can cut it down.'"

In these days of Lent we are talking and singing of the cross. *Singing* of the cross? Yes, that's just the glory of our faith—we can sing and make melody *about suffering and death*, about the sacrificial pain of God's Son on the tree, because the cross is God's mercy-giving second chance for all of us. In worship we come with the rest of God's people—confessing sins and admitting our waywardness, *and* receiving the news that a loving Father waits at the door to welcome us.

Prayer: Lord, the spirit among us here today should be so joyful, because each of us has experienced Your second chance. In Christ we are Your dear children. Because of the cross we know this. So help us to make our music an act of thanksgiving and a sharing of the fellowship we have through Your Son, Jesus Christ our Lord. Amen.

Prayer before worship: Lord God, now we must set everything aside and look only to the cross. Thank You for bringing us to this place today, where many others will gaze upon the cross with us. Help us all to see Your perpetual love in the work of Jesus Christ. Give us power to accept the way to which He is calling us today. Grant us now a joyful celebration of our hope in Christ. Amen.

Our Duty to God

Sometimes we may fall into the trap of believing that certain things we *do* make us God's acceptable people. Like singing in a choir!

Not that our music-making for the Lord does not please Him. Surely we pray that it does. But no one or two tasks, done in the greatest dedication, ever make us acceptable to the Lord.

The elder brother in the familiar parable of the prodigal son shows us as much. The younger boy took his rightful lot and lived irresponsibly—far away from duty to his father. The elder brother kept to home and remained duty-bound to his father.

Yet he was not hailed as a saint. You see, just doing the accepted godly chores (like choir singing!) does not make one acceptable in the Lord's sight.

What God truly desires is a heart that depends on no outward duties or words of our own at all, but solely on His grace and love. Today let each of us say, "I sing because I know the Lord has called me His child and I trust and believe His word. My song is not my ticket to grace, but *His* grace is rather my reason to break forth in song." So let us sing as free spirits under a Father's loving watch!

Prayer: O God, today our songs can be joyful, our music can be breeze-filled. For we have nothing else to do than to accept Your love in Christ and hold high His cross for all the world to see. Fill our hearts with such faith and zeal, O Lord. Do it now. Amen.

Prayer before worship: Lord, today again we are coming home, after a week in which we now desperately need Your grace and accepting arms. Cause us to trust in nothing else except Your familiar figure, standing with limbs outstretched to forgive and heal us all. In Jesus crucified, we pray. Amen.

Doing the Will of Jesus

The days of Lent move on in an ever-growing climax. Soon we will be worshiping our crucified Savior and risen Lord. Most of the music we now sing carries this strong theme of the suffering Savior's amazing love and His more amazing victory of Easter.

All of this is set in the context of our own fleeting time. The days run out. There is work to be done for God's kingdom. But always—always—Jesus is to be found doing the Father's will and the work of the Kingdom. During Lent we see Him most magnificently carrying out the sacred task.

And how about us? By His worthy suffering and victory, Christ is the head of His church. The master of the vineyard will return. Shall we be found doing His will?

The will of Jesus these days is precisely this welcoming of the suffering Savior when He comes among us. The cross is not attractive. The Son of God stretched out in suffering and pain is not our idea of a welcome guest. Why should we respect someone more poor and lowly than we? So we often reject the strong call to duty and noble living that His sacred head portrays. We become participants in His very crucifixion!

As the days of Lent run their closing course, let them not have been spent in vain. All our singing of the cross these days is the Savior's own invitation to us, "Take up the cross and follow Me!"

Prayer: Lord, we can become tired of speaking about and thinking about and singing about Your cross! Revive our hearts and minds now to see Your crucifixion boldly, so boldly that we do not shrink from it, but allow Your embracing arms to enfold us in its love, released again to take our own cross and follow You. Amen.

Prayer before worship: Today, O Savior, let nothing keep our eyes from looking upon Your suffering and death. Let nothing keep our hearts from believing that You love us. Today let nothing silence our lips from singing praise to You for saving us and keeping us. In Your name we pray. Amen.

Christ Crucified

"How to put Him to death!" This is the glorious, if somber, theme of Holy Week. In lengthy Bible readings, we shall hear the sacred record—in great detail—of how they put Him to death. "Christ crucified." That is the word for the coming days.

Somehow the worshiping church has always made this sacred story something *glorious* instead of tragic. Musical composers like J. S. Bach have written Lenten chorales and passion music that lift us to the heights of worship instead of holding us down in sentimental feelings of sorrow and tears.

That must be the spirit of our songs today! "Christ crucified!"—our *glorious* theme and the content of our message, because at the cross we shall see again rescue, deliverance, healing, and forgiveness. We shall see the royal Son, though crowned with thorns, crowned nevertheless. Salvation, life, and the very things that spell eternity are hammered out in His crucifixion.

So sing the songs firmly, with full vowels and undergirding breath. The Lamb of God leads all the way, and victory is in the air!

Prayer: Heavenly Father, as You sent forth Your Son as the Lamb of God who takes away the sin of the world, so send us forth as Your people, without fear or worry, to do Your will. Grant Your special blessing and strength to us all as we sing of Your great love and sacrifice. We pray in the name of our suffering Savior and King. Amen.

Prayer before worship: O Lord, today we enter Your sanctuary with profound penitence and hopeful faith. As Your Son goes forth to the passion and cross, grant us power to watch with Him and see the faithfulness He showed in all things. Give blessing to the preaching of the cross and bind us to Yourself and one another in the blessed sacrament. In Christ's name we pray, Amen.

Monday in Holy Week

Prayer before worship: Lord Jesus, You once entered Jerusalem to accept the Father's plan of suffering and pain for our salvation. Today we enter Your sanctuary here to again accept the saving rescue You won for us all. These are solemn days, O Savior, for we meditate upon Your passion. May we never shun the way of suffering and sacrifice to which our faith calls us, but give us ready hearts to bear all things in Your name. In this solemn week give special strength and grace to our leaders of worship, that the message of the cross may bear rich fruit in all our lives. Amen.

Tuesday in Holy Week

Prayer before worship: O sacred Head now wounded, we would enter Your sanctuary today to watch with You in Your suffering for a world of sin. As we look upon Your holy cross today, give us spiritual insights to see that it was all done for our good, that having peace within our hearts, we might be freed to serve others in our daily life in similar sacrifice, and one day, dying with Your name upon our lips, would inherit paradise forever. In Your blessed name we pray, O Christ. Amen.

Wednesday in Holy Week

Prayer before worship: Jesus, priceless treasure, hear our prayer in these holy days for Your church in all the world. As the blessed message of the cross is preached and taught in millions of places, may the hearts of many be turned to You, acknowledging You as the suffering Savior and the bringer of eternal life. May this be the good result of our meeting in Your name now, blessed Lord. Amen.

A Meal of Faith

Most of us are not too interested in eating when the pressure is on. Tense situations cause a loss of appetite. We don't know how things are going to turn out, and that's when the stomach begins to turn.

One can hardly imagine our Lord, then, being interested in a hearty, festive meal on Maundy Thursday! The chips are down. A brooding darkness closes in. He knows He is moving toward His death. How will *that* turn out? Even the Son of God had not experienced death yet! The whole situation was enough to cause a loss of appetite.

But in these words we read how Jesus went about deliberately—even confidently—preparing the Passover feast. He did it because He regarded this gathering with His friends as a meal of *faith*. Jesus did not forget what the Passover was all about. In former times God's people trusted the Lord to deliver them—and He did! His mighty acts delivered them from Egypt and all its bondage. The people put their faith in God and saw salvation and rescue.

Now Jesus ate *this* meal in such faith. The Father would deliver Him. The cross would not be the final word. So boldly did Jesus trust the Father in these moments that He gave the disciples His body as living bread. The act of His death on the morrow would bring nourishment and life to all believers for ages to come! So Jesus eats this meal in faith, and so do we.

Prayer: Lord Jesus Christ, I thank You for Your faithfulness to the Father's will. I thank You that You did not shrink from Your calling to bring salvation to all people. As I come to Holy Communion, may it be a meal of faith for me, pointing me to Your own body and blood, shed for me and given to me in this meal so that I may meet all the challenges and pressures of my life with Your power and aid. This I pray, O Christ. Amen.

Prayer before worship: Dear Savior, on this holy day in which You sat at meat with your friends, singing songs of praise, and sharing Your own body and blood through bread and wine; make of this a meal of faith for me and all who feast with me, that we may find in You strength for our lives and peace for our souls. As we sing our songs of faith, may the whole church be joined with us in praise of Your name, living with the Father and Spirit, our God forever! Amen.

A Lamb Goes Uncomplaining Forth

Today we have the overwhelming task of characterizing the whole event of Good Friday in a few words. So rich and varied is the message of the cross and crucifixion that down through the ages we have used several images or pictures in speaking of it.

We know one thing for sure: Good Friday is a climactic hour, the height of Jesus' saving work in our behalf. The plan of the Father is reaching its completion. That is part of the picture of Good Friday given to us in the solid Lenten hymn, "A Lamb Goes Uncomplaining Forth." As we read the lengthy Bible section above, we might give it this summary title: "A Lamb Goes Uncomplaining Forth."

The words impress us that Jesus is going forth to the cross on cue, in response to an eternal plan of mercy that the Father has for His dear children. Thus it is that Christ our Lamb goes forth to the cross *without complaint*. Though the suffering is no sham and the anxiety is bitter as can be, the Lamb accepts His role as Savior with a holy serenity that gives His entire death a glowing dignity. No unfortunate crucifixion, His! Rather Jesus has *agreed* to take up the cross and bear the shame.

Sometimes we complain about the time consumed in music rehearsal for our songs, the demands being made upon us during these days when choir and church schedules may be admittedly heavy. But really the complaints and the so-called sacrifices we make must fade into the background when we view the majesty of *this* willing suffering Servant, now bearing all things on the cursed tree. So let us sing our songs of His death with holy cheerfulness and humble thanks. Those who hear will then get the message, and Christ will be glorified!

Prayer: Jesus, Savior of the world, Lamb of God, have mercy upon us. Forgive our ill-will for not enthusiastically doing Your bidding and answering Your call. This Good Friday is a day we have been building up to for some time. Help us now not to miss its message: Your noble work of willingly saving us, and our grateful response of singing Your praise and giving glory to Your name with ready hearts. Hear us, O Christ. Amen.

Prayer before worship: Christ crucified, on this solemn day of Good Friday we come to Your house and into Your presence with unending thankfulness. Cast out of our hearts and worship any sentimentality or artificial sorrow, and cause us to see and sing of the majestic glory of the cross. Lift up our hearts and all who worship with us, that all may be enfolded in Your outstretched arms of love this good day. In Your holy name we ask it. Amen.

O Happy Day

When Georg Friedrich Handel was composing his famous choral work on the life of Christ, called *Messiah*, he came to a climactic spiritual moment in writing the "Hallelujah Chorus." His ecstasy at the vision of Christ's triumph was so great that he imagined heaven itself opened to his eyes, where he beheld the Lord in glory.

Such is the vision all of us may have on the feast of Easter. Christ is risen. O happy day! As it was for Handel, our dream is based on Biblical realities. The people who came to the tomb early on Easter did not find their Lord. He had risen. He was not in the grave.

His story becomes *our* story. That is why we say, "O happy day!" It is not only Christ's story, but ours. Death can no longer hold sway over us either! We are joint heirs with Christ of a glorious inheritance in heaven. If we need anything to set us to our musical tasks, we have it in the rising of the Son of God. Surely we do not wish for anyone to miss the aliveness, the sparkle, and the truth of the Easter message. So we give ourselves to words and music, hoping that some others will also see the heavens opened and the risen Lord sitting on the throne. What a high calling and noble work we have to do!

Prayer: O God of life and living, the Creator and Re-Creator, now the great day of deliverance is upon us! Your exodus from the grave in the rising of Christ has brought us eternal life. You have graciously led us through baptismal waters, and behold, we live! Grant that all our singing and making of music may be a profound celebration and acclamation of the victory over death to life which Christ has won for us all. We pray in His ever-glorious name. Amen.

Prayer before worship: O God, Father, Son, and Holy Spirit: this is the day You have made; we rejoice, and we are glad in it! Our role as singers in Your sanctuary today is doubly important, for the news of Easter is the grandest of all. So sweep our hearts and minds now of all sorrow and distraction, and plant the new song of joy within us. Alleluia! Praise to You, O living Lord! Amen.

The Peace of Easter

"Peace be with you!" That was the Easter greeting of Jesus Himself. To His own dear disciples He came with the word of encouragement, "Peace!"

That is the mood of our worship this Sunday: the peace of Easter. We all realize that it would be difficult to maintain the high pitch of last week's worship celebration. In these days of Easter afterglow we glory in the more quiet peace of Easter.

Again it was Georg Friedrich Handel who captured the mood for us. The jubilant "Hallelujah Chorus" in *Messiah* is followed by the soprano aria of serene confidence, "I know that my Redeemer liveth." The peace of Easter indeed! I know that Christ lives.

Today we do not meet behind any locked doors as did the disciples on that first Easter. We are not afraid. Jesus has given us everything we need to continue singing a song of triumph and peace.

Prayer: Thank You for the blessings of Easter, Lord. For its peace and serenity we praise You. Thank You for blessing our musical efforts in the important holy days now past. May we continue to sing the new song of Easter, not only in worship, but in our families and daily life always! Glory to You, O Christ. You reign with the Father and Spirit always! Amen.

Prayer before worship: Now Easter happens all over again, Lord, as You come to us here in Word and Sacrament today. As we hear Your word of peace, give us encouragement for the days of this new week. Bring us a new enthusiasm for Your work of missions in the world that all the world may see You as living Savior. Be present, Lord! Amen.

Swim for Life

We hope that none of us will ever find it necessary to swim for our life. But that is somewhat the picture portrayed in the Gospel event here.

Simon Peter, in a delightful show of enthusiastic faith, cannot wait for the boat to come to shore so that he can greet the risen Savior. In a moment of joy, he jumped into the water and swam for life. He swam to Him who is Life, our Lord Jesus Christ.

Yes, Jesus was crucified but now alive on this post-Easter day. Peter swam the one hundred yards to be with the Lord of life. A charming vignette of lively Easter faith!

Today Jesus the living one waits for our enthusiastic coming as well. Today let us sing our songs with extra life and vitality. Let us worship this Sunday with alert attention to the Easter Christ. Let us show our faith and demonstrate our zeal for the living Lord in all the ways we can. Christ will be glorified, and the world will know that we believe.

Prayer: Risen Savior, there is so much for us to be enthusiastic about in these happy days of the Easter season. We confess that our excitement over You cools too quickly and fades too fast. Stir us in our singing to Your name, that our hearts may leap and our lips may move in adoration of You who lives and reigns as risen Savior forever. Amen.

Prayer before worship: Heavenly Father, what a privilege it always is to come into Your presence! We come with thanksgiving and praise. We come in the name of the risen Savior, who has filled our lives with new hope and eternal dimension. Now we praise Him and sing for the glory of His name. Amen.

Our Divine Shepherd

The shepherd is a leader, and we need a leader. But the Good Shepherd, Jesus Christ, is much more than that. Not only is He our leader; He is our Savior as well.

Even the shepherd will lead the sheep at times through rough places—places that are dangerous and threatening. In such times more than a leader is needed. One who is able to meet the enemy and ward him off is the need then. One who is not fearful of the dangers involved in protecting the sheep is our deepest need then.

Jesus Christ is that kind of Shepherd! He endures every danger necessary to bring us through to life. He suffers every woe needed to maintain our safety and get us to green pastures again.

All of this saving activity we behold again in these Easter days. The suffering Lord has been more than a leader. He has been a Savior. So He was exalted, and so He was lifted up on the day of Easter victory. So we acclaim Him now as Shepherd King.

Prayer: Jesus, our divine Shepherd, always ready to hear our prayer, grant us grace now to worthily offer our chants and anthems of praise to You. Make them more than disciplined word and concentration, but make them that too, so that our song will be the best we can give You. Amen.

Prayer before worship: Savior, like a shepherd lead us. Give skill and insight and wisdom to those who lead us now in worship, that they may be faithful shepherds, pointing us to Your work of salvation and love. Hear us in Your mercy, Lord. Amen.

The Glory of Love

What makes for glorious music? There are always those folks who feel that the music must be loud and the forces making the music large in number if the goal of "glorious music" is to be achieved.

That would leave out most of our church choirs, no doubt. In these days when many choirs struggle for numbers, directors of music often feel happy to have as few as four or five in each voice section. Even having *one* tenor is sometimes regarded as a direct blessing from the Lord! It's obvious that grand choral forces are pretty much limited to the concert hall.

But our music can still attain the heights of glory! Not that which is big or loud is always "glorious."

The signals for *godly* glory are found in such themes as humility, service to others, purity, and a witness that always points to Jesus Christ and His self-giving love.

Some of the most "glorious" church music can be found in the quiet, measured organ preludes of Bach. The Gregorian chants (still used in our Christian worship today) are restrained, but capable of lifting us to heights of devotion and praise.

That is the "glory" of Jesus' love: He faithfully and quietly obeyed the Father's call as He laid down His life and was made alive again in the stillness of Easter dawn. One Lamb died for the people and comes alive again.

Whatever our musical forces may be, we have a faith in Christ that is able to make all our songs glorious. To that noble task we now give ourselves again.

Prayer: Lord, help me to see that one brief song, sung in love to Christ, is more glorious than any showy anthem, sung to our own praise. In Jesus' name. Amen.

Prayer before worship: This is the day of worship. This is the day of song. This is the day of gathering. This is the day the Lord gives us to magnify His name. Fill our worship with Your resurrected glory, O Christ, and help us in this hour to comprehend the vastness of Your love. And the peace of the Lord be with us all. Amen.

The Spirit Is Coming

When someone dear has been staying with us, we hate to see them go. The fellowship and good times we've had are precious in our minds. We hate to hear our dear one finally say, "Well, it's time to go."

In these words Jesus is saying just about that. "It's time to go. I leave you in peace. Don't get upset or sad over My going. In fact, be glad for Me. I am returning to My Father."

These parting words would have been unbearable for our Lord's disciples, except for one further fact. Jesus promised that after He left, the Holy Spirit would come. This would make Jesus' parting bearable, for it would be the Spirit's mission to bring the blessing of faith and belief to all who must walk alone in the world.

As we meet in these waning days of the Easter season, we may take heart. We are not alone! The Spirit of the Lord comes. He prompts our memory and fills our minds with faith as we recall the life of Jesus, His blessed death and cross, His victory-giving rising.

All that we have to do now, in our lives, and in service to Christ and His church, we can do with new vigor, for boundless faith and blessing are ours through the Holy Spirit!

Prayer: Lord Jesus Christ, we know that You have gone to the Father. But we know that You have not left us alone. Whenever we gather together as Christians to talk of Your love or to sing of Your rising, the Holy Spirit comes to us. He makes our hearts alive to You and brings us Your peace. So we thank You for our gathering here today. We have come together to say this in Your name. Amen.

Prayer before worship: All things are now ready, O Lord. The word is prepared. The songs are rehearsed. The meal is waiting. Now let Your Holy Spirit overtake all these preparations and make them a living revelation of Your grace and love. Grant these prayers in the power of Your Spirit, Lord Jesus. Amen.

Witnesses

The festival of Ascension is one of the gala days in the Christian worship calendar. It celebrates a culminating fact in the life of Jesus. He was born as Savior; His purpose was to "suffer and on the third day rise from the dead." Soon afterwards Christ could rightly return to the heavenly place, for as far as the Father's plan for man's salvation, Jesus had "gotten it all together."

The Ascension becomes a culminating event, then, as Jesus withdrew His physical presence from the earth and was taken up to heaven. Man's salvation is accomplished! Jesus sits down at the Father's right hand.

This story must now be told. This salvation news must now be shared. Those who have witnessed this saving activity of God in Christ are to *give* witness of it all to others.

As Christians this witnessing task can give purpose and depth of meaning to our choir singing. If our only purpose was to sing on key, or perform music too hard for the average person in the pew to do, then our goal would be shallow indeed. Or if we sing only out of loyalty to a director or even because we feel it our duty to support music in the church, then our songs may have little meaning, for us or for those who listen.

But Jesus says: "You are witnesses!" Yes—we have seen the King; and we proclaim the King. Ascension day calls us to this witnessing task in our daily living, our words, and our music in the church!

Prayer: Praise be to You, O Christ! All honor and praise are due Your name. You sit at the Father's right hand. All things have been placed under Your feet. You are the ascended Lord. Now we want to be your witnesses, so we ask for Your Spirit, that He might fill us with faith and freedom and fire. We pray for our congregation and our pastor(s), as all of us seek to proclaim Your victory to the world. Amen.

Prayer before worship: Lord Jesus Christ, we want to worship You on this special festival day. As You have risen to the heights, so in worship and praise raise us up now to heavenly places of adoration. Send us Your Holy Spirit, that He may show us even more of Your divine glory. We are praying in praise to Father, Son, and Holy Spirit. Amen.

Praying for Others

We may find it easy to pray for ourselves, but how about praying for others? There is no higher example of such prayer for others than our Lord Jesus Christ, praying here for His brothers and sisters in the world, in the moment when He Himself is about to go to suffering and shame in the ordeal of the cross.

In these verses of John 17 Jesus affirms His firm union with the Father. He exults in the love of the Father which is His. Now He prays that others may know similar divine love as He goes to the cross to reveal it.

In these Easter days, what an example Jesus gives us here! Not only are we called to pray for others and their needs. We are called *to be the answer* to the very prayers we ask for those around us. This lays it heavy on us. But it is the way of Christ. His cross became the answer to His own prayer for us. And now our acts of love—concern and sacrifice and selfless deeds—become the answers to our own prayers for others.

May we regard each other with such sensitivity and feeling now, met here as we are under the lordship of Christ the crucified!

Prayer: Heavenly Father, now we pray for others. Give us a sensitivity to the needs and desires of all who surround us in our daily lives. Grant us the selfless wisdom of Your Son to go forth in self-giving and sacrifice, that we might be the very answers to the prayers we say for others. In Jesus' name we pray. Amen.

Prayer before worship: Blessed Savior, You invite us to pray. You call us to ask for anything in Your name. Now give us grace to pray for others, for the needs of our sisters and brothers in the faith, for the conversion of all those who do not know You. Then give us courage, as in this service, to have Your name on our lips when we leave this place to do Your will. Amen.

The Counselor Is Here!

In these verses Jesus refers to the Holy Spirit as the Counselor. The message of this Sunday's festival is this: the Counselor is here!

How eagerly we look forward to celebrating this festival of Pentecost, for who of us wouldn't welcome some additional direction, some precise divine prodding as we live out our days in these challenging times.

The Counselor is such a directing Spirit. He gives us direction and guidance—in our lives, our church, and our worship. Life lived alone these days with only our own resources and whims, would be a grim prospect. The church of Jesus also needs His counseling power as it seeks to be His responsible instrument in a world gone off track. And how can we even worship this Sunday, or give our choral work any life or meaning, without this Counselor, this Spirit from on high?

So we look forward to this festival with joy and anticipation. The puzzle of life and faith has its pieces brought together in beautiful unity by the Holy Spirit of Christ Himself!

Hallelujah! Come, Holy Spirit!

Prayer: Holy Spirit, fire of love, bringer of faith in our blessed Savior, come. Be our Counselor in life, in church, in worship. Enflame our courage and hope, unite us in Your holy church, and make of us the true body of Christ on earth. Give such excitement to us even now as we celebrate with the kind of music that honors Christ, our Savior, and the Father's Son. Amen.

Prayer before worship: Hail, O festival day. Hail to You, O Spirit of the living Lord. Because Christ is risen, You have life to bring. Because we are victors with Him, You have hope to give. Because we are lost without Him, You have counsel to share. So hail the day that sees Your coming, blessed Spirit, sent by the Father, revealing our Savior. Make this an hour of fire, kindled by the Word, climaxed in the sacred meal of Christ's presence. Amen.

Guidance Needed!

People think they need guidance in life. And so they do. We all do. But in our religion it is ever so true: we need the divine guidance of God's Holy Spirit!

How else explain—or at least absorb—the mystery of this Sunday's festival, the Holy Trinity? Father, Son, and Holy Spirit! We sing of this blessed trinity so often in introits and other liturgical songs. But who can *know* this God or fathom the Three in One without some guidance from the Spirit?

The festival of Trinity is good for us. Not that it informs us any more about something we cannot understand. Rather, it presses us to realize that there is so much about our God and His ways that we will never know. There is nothing to do but accept Him. There is nothing to do—period. It is all His gracious work for us—and Jesus Christ has shown it all to us. So we sing for Him, not because we know all about Him, but because knowing little but His love and mercy, we can only offer our songs in grateful wonder and humble praise. May this be the spirit and the character of our music today!

Prayer: Father, Son, and Holy Spirit, all we know of You comes from You. We confess that faith is what we need the most: faith to accept the mystery of Your divinity and faith to know that Your wisdom is wiser than ours and always goes before us. Our gathering here is in Your name, so please accept the work we are about to do, that our lips may be singing Your praise. Hear us, blessed Trinity. Amen.

Prayer before worship: May the Father, who created us, sustain us for worship. May the Son, our Redeemer, be the word of good news on our lips, and may the Holy Spirit make living liturgy of each one here, as we now enter to give glory to our triune God. Amen.

The Glory and Help of Worship

"I am not worthy to have You come under my roof!" That is the sentiment of a humble soul who realizes that Jesus is approaching his door. Is it not also our plea as we come together for worship each week? Who is worthy of the Lord's presence?

But this is just the glory—and the importance—of our weekly Christ-centered celebrations! *Jesus is present in our midst.* The long haul is now upon us—more than two months of summertime worship in the Lord's house. But each occasion shall be a time of glory, for Jesus comes under our roof.

We are not only taken by the glory of it all. When Jesus comes, He always comes *to help.* To the centurion in the story it was a marvelous occasion when physical healing was brought to his house. So Jesus comes under our roof with help and healing as well. The glorious Christ is still the Man of the cross. He brings a healing of forgiveness as Savior of us all.

And with that there comes all kinds of further help and aid: courage for the day, peace for the mind, mending for the body, and a heart opened to the needs of all around us.

So with eagerness and expectation, let us be ready for the glory and help of worship that is ours again this Sunday, as Jesus comes under our roof!

Prayer: Lord, we pray that You would come and bring Your glory and help to this hour. Our purpose is to praise You. Our delight is to serve You. Our privilege is to welcome You as our divine guest. And so we do, O Lord. Amen.

Prayer before worship: Lord Jesus, we are not worthy that You should come under our roof. But we wish to share Your glory and to receive Your divine help. So come, Lord Jesus. Be now our guest. May this worship for all be blest! Amen.

It's Working!

We are trained to look for results. The sales manager wants salesmen who sell. The church officers want preachers who fill the pews. The baseball manager wants a pitcher who wins games.

And when we look at the public ministry of Jesus, filled as He was by the Holy Spirit, we may conclude, "It's working!" Yes indeed, it's working. The *Holy Spirit* is working in Jesus, and there are results. Here in the Bible verse a young man is raised to life again, and his mother feels richly blessed. All the people felt as much when they concluded that God Himself was visiting them in this prophet of Nazareth. It's working! *He* is working, and all is well.

Sometimes the working is slower, but we will continue to trust. The yeast that raises the bread works slowly. The medicine that we take for an illness may have effect only after several days or weeks. And when it seems that the work of Jesus is bogged down, resigned as He is to the cross and its bitter shame, then we will wait patiently for the light of Easter dawn. We will trust and believe that through the Holy Spirit Jesus is always at work—for our good!

Prayer: O Holy Spirit, give us faith to see Your gracious working not only in the pleasantries of life but also when questions and pressures edge against us. May we never doubt that in Jesus Christ the victory of life is always ours! In His name we pray. Amen.

Prayer before worship: O blessed hour, Lord, when we may sit at your feet and share Your grace and love! Give focus to everything here, Lord—the liturgy, the songs, the sermon, the sacrament, so that the Word of Your amazing salvation may break forth and fill us with renewed joy. In the Spirit's power grant it. Amen.

51

Sinned Much and Loved Much

Our devotion today bears the title, "Sinned Much and Loved Much." That is the story of your life and mine, isn't it so? Sinned much and loved much indeed! There is no doubt of our common sinfulness. "All have sinned and come short of the glory of God."

Yet we are also loved much. The center of the Christian message is just that. We are loved much—by a gracious heavenly Father. "God so *loved* the world that He gave His only-begotten Son." In the blessed saving work of Jesus' cross and victory, we are loved much, though we have sinned much.

So now, as Jesus suggests in this Bible story, a divine principle ought to emerge. In verse 47 Jesus says, "He who is forgiven little, loves little." The reverse positive result is our goal. If we have been greatly forgiven, then we ought to love much.

That's really the blueprint for the Christian life under the Spirit, isn't it? Realizing the profoundness of our forgiveness in Christ, we will practice the grace of love and forgiveness in our dealings with all others. May the Holy Spirit so overtake our lives that this pattern breaks forth daily in us!

Prayer: Lord, we have sinned much, and You have loved much. So we rejoice in this good news of Your grace. As we are now gathered in Your name, give us something of the wonder of it all, that our music and hymns may be offerings of gratitude and praise in the coming celebration of worship. Amen.

Prayer before worship: Lord, why are we here today? Because it is the Lord's day—a day only You could make, for Your day is always the day of hope and promise, of good news and love, offered and won by our Savior Jesus Christ, shared now among us in Word and Sacrament. So it is, and so we come. Amen.

Confession and Commitment

Confession is one thing. Commitment is another. In these verses Jesus seemed so aware of both. He eagerly desires our confession of faith, it is true.

In this interchange with the disciples He questions them as He presses them toward a clear confession of who He is. Peter typically answers for the others and says it so well. Who is Jesus? "The Christ of God," is the Rock-man's answer. How important that all of us can say that from the heart!

But Jesus immediately links confession to commitment. The next paragraph has Him addressing the Twelve: "If any man would come after Me, let him deny himself and take up his cross daily and follow Me."

In our setting here of singing for the Lord, the idea of Jesus works out like this: sing for the Lord, yes, but also have a song in your heart. That is to say, it's a fine thing to make music that honors the name of Christ and His mission. The confesion of faith we make regularly in song is good.

But have a song in your heart, too! See to it that the music on your lips is coming from within, from a deep commitment and loyalty to Jesus Christ and the Gospel news that He brings.

May there always be a song on our lips because there is first of all a song in our hearts!

Prayer: Lord Jesus Christ, only You can plant a song in our hearts— confidence and faith and trust because we know we are Your forgiven children. We thank You for this gift of faith, and ask You that the song on our lips may always reflect Your presence and love in our hearts. Amen.

Prayer before worship: Today we come here to say, "You are the Christ and our God forever!" Unite our hearts in this confession of faith, Lord, and give us grace and power to act upon it in the days of this new week. For the glory of Your name we pray. Amen.

Being Under a Master

Most of us could accomplish greater things in our lives if we were more single-minded. Even today we could have produced more results if our goals and purposes had been given greater focus. Often our commitments are too widely scattered.

When it comes to fulfilling God's will and following the Savior's way, this single-mindedness is essential if we are truly to serve Him. Jesus says as much in the rather harsh-sounding words of this Sunday's Gospel. "Leave the family funeral and don't even take time to say farewell to those at home. Just come and follow Me. Once you set your eyes on Me and My will, look at nothing else."

These statements by our Lord are meant to impress us with the Kingdom's demands. All work for Jesus and His church calls for our utmost concentration and discipline. Christians are not free-floating spirits. They are under a master. And it is the Lord.

Part of the kingdom work for which Christ has chosen us is church music. Admittedly there are other attractive activities to divide our minds these summer days. But for now we will put ourselves beneath director and music and the goal of enriching the worship of Christ's people. In doing so Christ Himself will bless our efforts and use us for deepening the influence of His kingdom here. O happy subjects we, under the lordship of the Master.

Prayer: There is much we can do here, O Lord, in Christian music and song. As we focus our minds now upon the sacred task, use our forces to create the beauty of Your salvation in the hearts and minds of all who will share in our efforts of song. In the Master's name we pray. Amen.

Prayer before worship: Lord, set our minds now on just one truth: the love and mercy You have shown in Christ, so that this hour may be a true celebration of the saving good news we know in His death and rising. Grant us this for Christ's glory. Amen.

Few Faithful Workers

Jesus says that there is a lot of work to be done in the Kingdom. He also says there are few workers for the job. Few faithful workers!

Jesus may not just be complaining about a lack of numbers here. He may also be saying that among the numbered workers in the church, few seem genuinely faithful. Isn't it so in any Christian congregation? Often there may be workers in the church, but not always *workers who follow through*. More than one enthusiastic worker for the Lord has been disillusioned along the way. How quickly we can run out of steam, with our zeal for doing a good job of God's work quickly evaporating.

So in application to our calling as singers in this choir, we may say, don't just *be* in a choir, be *dedicated* to it. Be one of the laborers who labors. Set your mind on the words; give attentiveness and silence when they are due. Be a *valuable* member of this ensemble. Heaven knows, Jesus is looking for that kind of worker here today and in every other part of His kingdom enterprise.

Prayer: Heavenly Father, You have highly valued us as You brought us into being through creation and then gave us new life in Your Son, Jesus Christ. May we now be valuable instruments in Your service, Father, as we accept the call of Your Son and do the work of the Kingdom with faithful, loyal hearts. For this work now, give us such zeal also. In Jesus' name we pray. Amen.

Prayer before worship: Blessed Lord, we thank You for faithful pastors and ministers who serve us in worship today. Grant them health and energy, joy and fulfillment in their ongoing work. Keep them as faithful laborers in the harvest. May this time of worship bear much fruit in the life and work of our congregation. You are our Savior, and we pray in Your name. Amen.

The Good Old Good Samaritan

Everybody knows about the good old Good Samaritan. That may be just our problem as we hear this reading in the service this Sunday. The familiar facets of the story fail to move or challenge us anymore.

A similar fate awaits all those aspects of our worship and religious life that become too familiar. The liturgy becomes innocuous in its regularity. Hymns lose their punch because we have many of the lines memorized. Even our choir anthems can suffer from over-rehearsal.

But when we really give the problem a second look, we usually discover that the loss of freshness and vitality in our listening and response lies somewhere else.

We plainly miss out on the amazing *freshness* of the message itself. The Good News is really news. Christ and His love for us is a living love, hammered out in suffering and pain on the tree. The word Life is given a capital letter "L" when we see the suffering Savior now standing alive in victory on Easter morn.

So with the Christian life and worship that follows. *Do* as the Good Samaritan did. Go two and six and ten extra miles for the good of the neighbors who touch your life each day and week. *Then* you will come to worship, and liturgy and songs and choir rehearsals and *this parable*—and they will all LIVE, for God's Holy Spirit will have been working within you!

Prayer: Gracious Lord, we confess that much of our religious piety and practice is way too familiar. The life and freshness have gone out of our faith when we have failed to allow You to lead us to venturesome service and living in Your name. Give us a pentecostal pouring of Your Spirit into our hearts now as we look to Your Son and our Savior, Jesus Christ. Then make everything in our religion alive again. Amen.

Prayer before worship: Lord Jesus, today we thank You that Your familiar figure welcomes us to worship as we come into Your house. We come with hope, with faith that You will transform our struggles to victory, our listening to insight, our worship to adoration, our seeking to a revelation of Your glory. Amen.

Distracted?

One characteristic word stands out in this short Gospel reading. The word is "distracted." We read that Martha was *distracted* with much serving. All of us, in our human ways and habits, can be distracted from what is good and what leads to good.

Not everything is always to be considered a negative distraction. Food and serving and gourmet enjoyment have their place. But in comparison with other opportunities they fade into the background. Surely one would choose listening to the Bread of Life over eating bread at some table!

We get to see that maybe this is the story of our lives— missing out on the better opportunities life has to offer because we are distracted by less important attention-getters.

In the frolic and change of pace that beautiful summer days have to offer, quite a few people almost forsake worship in church and the sacraments. We begin to hear all kinds of unusually solemn talk about the Lord's presence in nature and about our ability to worship Him in our hearts, apart from the congregation.

In such times we are plainly distracted. We are forsaking the larger opportunity of the encouraging fellowship, healing, and forgiveness to be found in corporate worship and are distracted by promises of rest and a new mind-set that vacations and outdoors are supposed to give.

It is hoped that we as Christians will be able to handle both opportunities with responsibility in these summer months, so that having Christ and His renewing fellowship in our hearts we will be able to enjoy all the beauties and pleasures of His good world!

Prayer: Jesus, You are the Bread of Life. Your nourishment for our faith never fails, for You are Your own gift to us. Give us grace to exult in all Your daily blessings. May we now set aside everything that would distract us from offering a pleasing song to Your praise. So bless us in our desire to serve You. Amen.

Prayer before worship: Now we have this hour to sit at Your feet, O Lord. May nothing distract us from hearing the Good News. Send Your Holy Spirit to open our hearts, giving us receptive wills to follow Your way. In Your blessed name we pray. Amen.

Prayer, Faith, and the Holy Spirit

All three subject matters of our title receive sterling treatment (as they always do) from the lips of our Lord in this reading.

Jesus talks about *prayer* by giving His disciples a prayer to pray. The high example of the Lord's Prayer is the world's finest verbal treatment of the whole subject!

People pray, Jesus seems to be saying as He goes, because they possess *faith*. The parable He tells of the midnight visitor has come to be a prime Biblical story of persistent faith and the joyous answer in response to that faith.

All is tied together as Jesus mentions the gift of the *Holy Spirit*, the valued treasure for which we all need to pray, because He is the bringer of faith.

We are not just choir singers. We are not just giving an acceptable musical rendition. We are people of Christ. Our song and music take place in the context of God's people, gratefully gathered for joyful hearing of the Good News and celebration of new life in Christ.

So it seems that we are also to be setting a premium on these three: prayer, faith, and the Holy Spirit. So we begin today in prayer. Faith is the substance of our petition, that, having the Holy Spirit within, we shall be able to truly glorify God in song!

Prayer: O heavenly Father, we pray because we have faith that You hear us. Our faith is the work of Your gracious Holy Spirit in us. All of this has been revealed by Your Son, Jesus Christ, who teaches us to pray, who encourages us to believe, who sends us the Spirit of truth. All praise to His name, who dwells with the Spirit in You, our God forever! Amen.

Prayer before worship: The time of meeting is here, O Lord. You meet us in Your Word and Sacrament. We meet You in the worshipers who come together with us, confessing their sins and telling of their needs. Grant us grace to serve You as we meet the needs of all who cry to You for help today. In Jesus' holy name we pray. Amen.

Rich Toward God

This is one of the most dramatic parables ever uttered by Jesus. It is so because of the deeply serious nature of the subject, the eternal fate of a man's soul. In a concluding remark about that subject, Jesus introduces us to one of His most succinct and important thought patterns, that of being *rich toward God*.

"Rich toward God!" What a challenge Jesus lays to our soul's imagination in that phrase! You and I are rich in many respects. We have our share of creature comforts. We are rich in knowledge about a lot of things, whether it be the latest statistics about our favorite major league ball team or an advanced appreciation of the musical cantatas of Johann Sebastian Bach.

But to be "rich toward God!" To know not just about Him, but to know *Him*. Surely it all involves a living relationship with Jesus Christ, the one who gave us these parables about the soul. For to be in tune with Christ is to experience His revealing to us of the Father and His love. As we look to the cross of Jesus and at the Lord risen and alive in Easter victory, we come close to knowing all the truths of faith that make us rich toward God.

Being rich toward God, through Christ, we can come more closely to offering a song of praise that truly calls God's people to a greater commitment of solid faith in the Lord.

Prayer: We thank You, Lord Jesus, for Your gracious revelation of the Father's love and mercy. You have made us rich toward God. Continue this good work in us by the aid of Your Spirit, as You show us the saving acts of Your death and rising. In Your name we pray. Amen.

Prayer before worship: We come as those who possess nothing, O Lord, and as those who need everything. Cleanse us in confession, confront us in Your Word, and feed us for spiritual strength in Your blessed sacrament, for we pray in Your name, who died for us and rose again. Amen.

What Are You Ready For?

What are you ready for? Most of us are ready for what we *want* to be ready. We're never quite ready for the test at school or the report at the office. Hard work and discipline are demanded for that! But when it's off on a vacation or holiday, most of us are ready and waiting.

The parable of Jesus in Sunday's Gospel speaks about our readiness to be committed to God's kingdom and to the work involved in extending it. Our mission in song can be considered part of proclaiming and extending this divine kingdom. What are we ready for?

A lot of small things add up to making some endeavors either signficant or mediocre. Choir rehearsals, for instance, are better when everyone arrives on time. They become increasingly better when all the singers listen carefully to requests of the director: getting the appropriate piece of music in hand, ready to sing; having an attentive ear to technical verbal directions, etc. In short, all the small disciplines of making music, faithfully carried out, give us a readiness to perform in a superior manner. And there is certainly nothing wrong with doing our best when it comes to the worship of God's house! Now let us be about this noble work of making a joyful noise to the Lord.

Prayer: Lord, all of us have days filled with important activities and concerns. And now it is time to offer our anthems of praise to You. Give us strength, wisdom, and alertness to be ready for our sacred task. In Your holy name we pray. Amen.

Prayer before worship: Blessed Lord and God, the day of the Son has come again, and we are ready to praise Him as our resurrected Lord. May we treasure this opportunity to gather as Your people, in Your house. May the message of the cross and empty tomb be the crowning beauty that pervades everything we do here now. Hear us for Jesus' sake. Amen.

A Religious Fanatic

One is almost tempted to read this whole Bible text a second time. It is hard to believe that the words are coming from our beautiful Savior and serene Master.

Perhaps we have considered Christ in terms too polite, unwilling to face the Gospel writer's portrait, which strongly suggests a *radical* Lord. Indeed does not Jesus here almost come across as a religious fanatic?

You and I draw away from any suggestions of fanaticism. But it is plainly true that such is the case with our Lord as we confront Him in this text. He is a man on fire.

There is a proper kind of fanaticism, of course, and that is what we discover here. Jesus is urgent in wanting to fulfill His duty toward other human beings. He feels pressed and pressured to get on with the divine work of salvation for which He was anointed as Messiah. For these good goals He contains a fanatical urge.

Indeed, so successful would be His work of rescue and saving, that persons within families would be swept away from traditional loyalties and would follow Christ with absolute commitment and obedience. The loyalty and dedication which some would give to the Gospel message would be enough to cause unrest and division wherever the proclamation was uttered.

Thank God for the vigorous faithfulness of the Savior in bringing us our rescue at the cross. May our enthusiasm to accept the Gospel and live by it be just as overwhelming!

Prayer: Lord, with our middle-of-the-road attitudes, it may be difficult to grasp Your single-minded purpose in accomplishing our salvation and bringing us to eternal life. Set in us a vision of the greatness of our faith, that nothing and no one would ever keep us from wholeheartedly believing and living it. We pray in the power of the Holy Spirit. Amen.

Prayer before worship: O Christ, O Christ of cheer and challenge, we do not always realize the radical nature of Your word and call. Give us grace in our worship now to listen to what You are saying. Then give power to believe in You and do what You ask of us. Thus will our worship ring true, and Your name will be glorified. Hear us, O Christ. Amen.

The Tables Turned

Who really knows what the score is? Especially when it comes to judging the worth of other people and what they are doing! It's a dangerous business, and Jesus warns against it often. Judge not. You may be dead wrong.

So we read in the closing words of the Bible verse here. Jesus says that some are last who will be first and some are first who will be last. Surprising results! A sobering thought indeed. Our call, then, is not to be judging what others are doing, but to be constantly striving to enter by the narrow door ourselves. Part of that discipline is to so realize that all our salvation rests completely on God's mercy in Christ, that it would be presumptuous for us even to suggest that, according to our observations, someone else might be muffing it spiritually.

So glorify Christ in your life by becoming a humble beggar spiritually so that there would be no possibility of your becoming trapped by the game of tables turned!

Prayer: Lord Jesus Christ, if we are going to rise above the game of judgment of others, we will need to know that even You do not judge us, but You love us and forgive us. This we know, when we think of it, as we recall Your bitter shame at the cross and Your surprising victory on Easter. Now we are free, and so can everyone else be, if our word to them is not one of judgment but of love. Help us do it, Lord. Amen.

Prayer before worship: Heavenly Father, we thank You for the good word of forgiveness we have in Your Son, Jesus Christ. His is the word we celebrate now, speaking it to one another and sharing it in His meal. May Your Holy Spirit guide us to experience all of this for the enrichment of our faith. Amen.

No Room for Pretense

Jesus has a way of zeroing in on the heart of the matter. He is good at uncovering our pretenses. He uncovers the secret motives for taking some of the actions we do.

Like being kind and hospitable to others, for instance. Isn't it true that you and I are often polite to others because that's what's expected of us? It's the old story, as Jesus observes, of inviting someone to dinner because we will then be repaid with an invitation to their table.

Then Jesus gets to the point. Would any of us have a dinner party for the dregs of society and the pitiful people in our urban areas—all the folks who turn us off? Probably not. Why not? Our mercy and love do not stretch that far. There's no recognition in it for us, so why bother? Jesus really lays bare our utter self-centeredness and sin.

But He doesn't do it for vicious reasons. He wants us to see, in contrast, the way that *God* loves. To His table of good things the Lord has invited poor you and me, spiritually poverty-stricken and unattractive as we are in our souls. Christ Jesus dies for us and rises again. Yes, for us!

So now we go forth, in humble heart, with a similar love to all, unshackled by thoughts of reward or notice by others. May this be the spirit and tone of our gathering now—humble hearts, grateful to be called sons and daughters of the King!

Prayer: Our merciful Savior, there are many needs we have and feel in our hearts as we meet together in Your name. But no need is greater than the gift of a humble heart—to see Your love, to see others in need of our love. So give us hearts that bow before You. Make ours the music of divine love. In Your saving name we pray. Amen.

Prayer before worship: All creation chants Your praise, our God. Flowers and fields, creatures and people show Your goodness in the world. May our worship now also truly praise You, without pretense, but with heartfelt adoration for the love we know You have shown us in Jesus Christ, our Lord. Amen.

How Come the Crowd?

How would we go about drawing a crowd of sincere followers, if we had to? Would we say what Jesus says here? "Whoever of you does not renounce all that he has cannot be My disciple." That's what Jesus says, and we read further, "Great multitudes accompanied Him." Fantastic! It seems unbelievable that such demanding words would be inviting to anyone. Renounce *all* that we have?

Obviously some of the crowd was sincere, and others were not. Maybe a few bit off a bigger chunk than they could chew. With enthusiasm they renounced all and began to follow the Master. But soon they discovered that they could not get along without the old familiar crutches of a faithless world.

The words of Jesus here are hard-hitting, designed to set us in a tailspin of inner spiritual inquiry. There is little we can do but pray for God's renewing Spirit, whose power we absolutely need at all times if we are to continue following our Savior as His faithful disciples. We earnestly pray this day for the gift of such grace, that Christ may always have first place in our lives.

Prayer: Jesus, our Lord, the demands and conditions of Your kingdom are so over-powering, we know we can never measure up to them except as You Yourself shall accomplish it all in us. So come, Lord Jesus, send the fire of Your Spirit to our souls, to consume us in loyalty and devotion to Your will and way. In trust we pray. Amen.

Prayer before worship: We come to worship for many reasons today, O Father. Some are overwhelmed by life and problems. Others are full of praise for the divine aid they have experienced from Your hand. In whatever mind we come today, O Lord, cause us to see that You can do everything for us and that any good in our life has come from Your loving hand. So bless our words and songs of praise. Amen.

What Are You Glad About?

Maybe we can get the true measure of a person by ascertaining just what it is that makes him glad. What are *you* glad about? What happenings truly make you happy?

In His usual accurate way, Jesus sizes up a situation as He observes the religious leaders becoming indignant over His unqualified reception and acceptance of commonly known sinners. In the beautiful parables that follow, Jesus is wondering why God's mercy and love shouldn't really be making them *glad*.

But how could it, when these Pharisees and scribes were filled with self-consciousness and a false sense of superiority? How could they possibly be glad when even one sinner is found by the loving arms of the Savior?

What makes us glad? Hopefully the loving and accepting heart of Christ that has even enfolded *us* in its warmth is what makes us joyful today. And more than that, pray God we are glad for each other, in this fellowship of music, knit together as we are under the redeeming love of Christ.

Prayer: Jesus, Lord of joy, there is much in life to make our hearts glad. There is little that should leave us indignant and bitter. May we always rejoice in the extension of Your kingdom and the saving grace that comes to every one of Your children. Make of us today a grateful fellowship of believers, glad for each other and thankful for our common faith in You. Amen.

Prayer before worship: Christ, Savior, thank You for planting a song of joy in our hearts today. Now bring this joy to the surface in the anthems of praise that we sing to Your name. Hence, fear and sadness; enter joy and gladness, into this holy house and within every heart gathered in Your name. Amen.

Keen for the Kingdom

There are a lot of subtleties in this Gospel that could keep us in discussion for a long time. But perhaps the prime meaning that the Lord would have us see could be wrapped neatly in the title phrase, "Keen for the Kingdom." Jesus is saying to us here, "Be as keen for the sake of My kingdom as you are in other enterprises of your life."

How keen we can all be when it comes to solving our own problems and supplying our own needs. We can be downright clever and resourceful then.

Jesus asks us to use the same lively imagination in service to His work and enterprise. Not being dishonest or crafty, to be sure, but giving the best of ourselves and our intelligence to help His kingdom come.

Today we can be thankful for all of those who have used the gift of music to create a constant variety of sound to praise the Lord. We can stand in amazement at the way the church has used radio and television, printing arts and varied architecture to serve in the mission of making Christ and His message known and noticed in our society.

More power to you, too, as you innovate and practice new forms of loving and serving, of sacrificing and giving, all for the sake of Christ's kingdom.

Prayer: O Lord, the world You have given us is one of never-ending variety. It's made our life so interesting each day. Now give us keenness and courage to share the message of Your love and mercy in many ways that will bring others under Your lordship. Your Spirit can do it all, O Lord, so we pray for His presence now and always. Amen.

Prayer before worship: Lord, You showed great inventiveness in bringing us salvation. For while we deserved Your condemnation, You went to the cross and died for us. When Your judging power should have held sway, You submitted to the weakness of Calvary. We are amazed by Your will to save us, Lord. May this service of worship be part of our grateful response for all Your undeserved love. In Christ's name. Amen.

What Does It Take?

Sometimes we are tempted to believe that a spectacular divine revelation would convert the world. Just what such a spiritual happening would consist of we're not sure. But we think it would work.

The only trouble is—it won't. Jesus made that clear in the Gospel appointed for this Sunday's worship. The rich man doomed to hellfire at least had a heart for his five living brothers. If a spectacular scene could be arranged in which Lazarus would appear to them from the dead, surely they would get the message and be converted.

But then Abraham gives the word. He says in effect that all it takes is the faithful, clear preaching of the Word, such as one could readily find in Moses or the familiar prophets of old. If God's living, powerful Word can't do it, no ghost from the dead can either.

So in this incident the Lord is suggesting no false style for our work of mission and ministry either. As singers of the Lord's song, we may sometimes be tempted to imagine that only the flashy, the relevant, or even the loud will convince and communicate a message that transforms.

But let no false hopes lead us on. *Whatever* our songs, faithfully prepared, sung from the heart, and done in humble worship of the Savior, they may be part of what the Holy Spirit uses to quietly do His work of renewal in the waiting soul. So let us do our music-making with faithfulness, and God will use us, to be sure.

Prayer: Lord, there is nothing so mysterious about Your work to be done on earth. The Word is proclaimed, the Spirit comes, and people are saved. Keep us from imagining that anything we contrive can outstrip the blessed Word of Life shared in speech and sacrament. Give us contentment in simply singing Your songs in faith and hope. Amen.

Prayer before worship: Blessed God and Father, there is no word of power, except the message of the cross of Your Son. Give delight to our hearts and souls now as we glory in the weakness of the cross and its power to save. This we pray in Jesus' holy name. Amen.

Our Duty—and More

The tendency we have is to believe that our deeds, after all, will win us God's approval. Though it may pain us, Jesus has to root out that idea from our spiritual thinking and aspiration. He lays us low in this Bible text here when He suggests that after all is said and done, we really do nothing to contribute to our state of salvation. Whatever you do, Jesus says, can only be considered your duty. It has no effect upon God's approval or disapproval of your entrance to the Kingdom. There is no surplus to give you extra credit.

Jesus is always making a point of this because the way of God's grace is strange to us. In fact, we cannot understand it at all. That's why it's grace. It's altogether God's idea and His work. Oh, painful word—*you* are not involved at all! Here at last is something you could not do.

That makes God all the greater, doesn't it? And His love in Christ comes off all the more profound. A pervading sense of thankfulness begins to emerge from our souls as we taste the full richness of the Lord's cup.

St. Paul was right: "By grace you have been saved through faith; and this is not your own doing, it is the gift of God—not because of works, lest any man should boast."

Prayer: God, make even our stance of prayer today a sign of our utter dependence on You for all things. Help us always do our duty. And then help us even more to realize that what we have done is *only* our duty. Salvation and new life is Your unique gift to us. Praise and glory, God, in Jesus' name. Amen.

Prayer before worship: Eternal is Your mercy, Lord, but now You break into our time in the Gospel of Your Son, Jesus Christ, the Savior. Today we feast on His love, share His new song, and enter Your presence without fear, but with joy. May this be our hour of worship, Lord. Amen.

The Need to Say Thank You

We can hardly blame them for forgetting. These ten lepers had not only a physical burden eradicated, but a social stigma lifted as well. No more leprosy meant a return to normal life in a free community. It was all overwhelming.

So they forgot to return thanks. They forgot to pay tribute to the Master who had made it all possible. The one leper who did remember received praise by Jesus. He reminds him to remember that it was all a matter of faith.

Jesus says in effect that this is the way it is all through life—the exciting life these ten were now to take up: when all is said and done, faith informs us that a gracious God is acting in our behalf. All good things come from His hand.

There is a need to say thank you, precisely so that our listing of thanks be the outward sign and confession that God does all the good among us and faith is the realization of His power and might in our own lives.

Today let us clear our hearts and minds of all personal claims and breathe a prayer of thanks for the privilege and ability to praise the Lord in song and music!

Prayer: Lord, let us see prayer as a privilege You have given, based upon all Your rich spiritual and physical blessings in our lives. Because of Your grace and love we really have something to think and thank about. So we say, now thank we all our God! Amen.

Prayer before worship: Blessed Jesus, You have healed us and You have saved us. We have returned to Your house today to give thanks. May our thanks center in an exultation of Your death and rising as we hear Your word and share Your meal. Feed us richly in this hour. Then send us out to serve You. Amen.

Keep Practicing!

We tell our children, and sometimes we need to tell ourselves: "Keep practicing!" Son or daughter just can't master an involved passage in the piano lesson. Keep practicing! Don't give up!

And such is the message of this Sunday's Gospel, too. It is a call to persistent prayer. It is an invitation to believe that faith in the Lord never need be abandoned. It is always worth storming the gates of heaven.

"Keep practicing" is just the encouragement we may need as we join in preparing the Lord's song. After all, this Sunday is so ordinary. Not Christmas, or Ash Wednesday, or Easter Sunday. Just the Twenty-second Sunday After Pentecost! Is my attentiveness and enthusiasm really going to matter? Shall I *have* to give myself wholeheartedly to this now?

Remember who it is that told the parable. Remember Jesus Christ. He is the one who is encouraging you to "keep practicing!" He deserves our best response—always. He is present every Sunday from altar, pulpit, and lectern. He comes to us in His Supper.

The prospects for healing, new starts, and forgiveness are exciting. Never an ordinary Sunday when Christ joins us in the midst of our salvation celebration! So we practice and keep on practicing, knowing that the Lord will bless and use our best efforts done in His name.

Prayer: Jesus, dear Savior, we sometimes have to admit that our music-making and song-preparing can be a task long-drawn. We need Your promise and Your spirit to encourage us. Lord, we have Your promise that You hear our prayers, so send us the Spirit of Pentecost and fill our songs with life! Amen.

Prayer before worship: Heavenly Father, this is no ordinary Sunday, for in Word and Sacrament You are filling Your people with Your life-giving presence. Cause excitement to run high among us, for this hour of worship is a meeting of Your people and a celebration of Your love. Amen.

False Humility

It's not that the tax collector was humble and the Pharisee was proud. Not at all. A careful reading of the parable convinces us that both were men of sincere religious intent. They possessed humility.

But the Pharisee had a false humility. He *trusted* in his humility. And that was fatal. For to trust in one's own humility is no humility at all.

In contrast, as Jesus sets up these characters, the tax collector did not trust in his humility; he trusted in God. That is never fatal, but always brings life.

Why so? Because trusting in God is banking on Him completely. It is forgetting—forsaking—ourselves. And that always means life. Trust opens up the way for God to enter our lives fully. And where God comes, there is life.

So how is it with us today? False humility or true? As soon as we begin enumerating what we have done—or not done—the game is over. We have made a god of our own humble stance. And well we know: "You shall have no other gods before Me."

Prayer: Lord Jesus Christ, the virtue of humility is so beautiful—and so treacherous. Thank You for pointing out the pitfalls. But now come, O Christ, and fill our lives, for You are the only one who can give us the grace of true humility. Amen.

Prayer before worship: We have this song to sing, O Lord. We have this prayer to pray. Only You can make our acts of worship acceptable in Your sight. So come and fill us with Your Spirit. He will grace our songs and guide our prayer, and all the glory will be Yours! Amen.

Surprise Guest, Surprised Host

This is the story of a surprise guest and a surprised host. Zacchaeus never dreamed of having Jesus Christ as a guest in his home. Evidently Zacchaeus was interested in this rabbi, and probably respected Him highly. That's why he, an executive tax collector, went out of the way to catch a glimpse of this man who seemed to stir the crowd.

The whole course of events therefore becomes doubly charming. Jesus announces to Zacchaeus that He feels compelled to call at his house that very day. As a popular religious leader, Jesus has an interview with a man who might most quickly ruin His public image!

It's a case of a surprise guest and an even more surprised host. But this is typical Jesus practice. Where we least expect Him to go, He goes. Those who least expect His coming receive the grace and favor of His visit.

Again the story tells us that all the old religious clichés are out. Christ comes purely out of grace—to those who cannot possibly have any claims to religious accomplishments or superiority.

Give you any hints?

Prayer: Heavenly Father, the lesson is clear. Your Son comes to all who claim nothing and need everything. Make us such worthy souls. Then we will have a spiritual right to join in these songs of praise, about the only gift we can really give You. Father, You know we are praying in Jesus' name. Amen.

Prayer before worship: Blessed Jesus, we are the guests and You are the host. Sometimes we would think it is the other way around. But only You, O Lord, are truly acquainted with the things of the Spirit. So lead us as guests in the mansions of Your presence. Let our worship be truly awe-struck and full of wonder at Your mercy and leading in our lives. In praise of Father, Son, and Spirit we pray. Amen.

Twenty-Fifth Sunday After Pentecost

The Life to Come

As was usually the case, the Pharisees missed the whole point about the glory of religion as Jesus came to reveal it. And so do we. How many times haven't we all engaged in idle talk about what it will be like in heaven. Rather presumptuous on our part!—assuming automatically that we will be there to observe it all, and then injecting the whole scene with our earthly allusions and finite ideas! Little better than the Pharisees—we.

In the verses here Jesus must once again patiently cast aside our proud human assumptions and remind us that heaven is such a stupendous, unimaginable gift, completely devoid of man's idea and filled with God's, that all our speculations about it are only a confirmation of our creaturely limitations and that we have yet to be made into angels.

Far more should we be concerned about the great events on earth that will one day usher us all face to face with the Lord of glory. God is a God of the living, not of the dead. Are we sure of our own ascension to life in the last day? We may be, thanks to Christ and His cross and to His glorious rising. Let us speculate on the glory of *that*, and one day heaven will be shown us too.

Prayer: Christ who came from heaven, we would go to heaven, and inherit all that the Father has waiting for us. In these closing days of the church year, focus our minds on the end, not in fear and anxious outlook, but in faith and joy. You will so encourage us, O Christ, we pray. Amen.

Prayer before worship: Our cycle of worship is ending, O Lord, and so is the world. May the thoughts of heaven that fill our worship these weeks instruct us about the passing of our own time and the grace of Christ which will bring us to the full life above. Make this the triumphant theme of our church service now! Amen.

Even Institutions Fall

Once again Jesus proves that He never took a Dale Carnegie personality course. As some of the respectable citizens of Jerusalem were caught in a moment of pride and ecstasy by the beauty of the Temple and its adornments, Jesus walked up and told them to look while they could. "As for these things which you see," He said, "the days will come when there shall not be left here one stone upon another that will not be thrown down."

Jesus was telling them not to place their chief energies and devotions in institutions. After all, institutions fail and fall, as would this Temple in A.D. 70.

The chief concern of the godly, Jesus would suggest, ought to be investments made in service to God and our fellowmen. Such investments of time and devotion, and of authentic response to God's Word, cannot be destroyed, nor can any who do such works have them harmed or destroyed. Jesus puts it triumphantly: "Not a hair of your head will perish. By your endurance you will gain your lives."

What a magnificent—and honest—Savior we have. The trappings and trials of institutional churches will come and go, but on the last day we shall be prepared for the Lord's questions, if we have put all our stock in the love of Christ and His forgiveness—a mercy and grace that moved us on earth not to trust in buildings but to be on the streets, serving and loving where we could.

Prayer: Christ, we know we may trust You. You always deal with us in honesty. You do not mislead us or give us false hopes. We know that the world will one day end and that You will come again. But we do not have to fear, because our future is in Your hands. You will bring us to heaven and we shall praise You, with the Father and the Spirit, our God forever. Amen.

Prayer before worship: Today we contemplate the end of all things, O Lord, in the joint worship we are privileged to share now. It is a fantastic theme and a necessary one, for all things draw to a close, and we are face to face with You. In Christ we shall stand, and the glory of the Kingdom will be shown to us. May we sing and pray and speak with such confidence now, O Lord. Amen.

Proclaiming Christ King

This Sunday is the festival of Christ the King. It is also the last Sunday of the current church year. As we look forward to our worship, the following theme emerges: all things are drawing to a close; the only truth that finally matters is that Jesus Christ is King.

Many songs in our liturgy and hymns in our worship books point us to the end of things. The Christian's ultimate goal is to one day be singing, "Holy, Holy, Holy" with the saints and angels above. Our own life and the span of this world's existence is drawing to a close.

We face this reality not in somberness but in joyful affirmation that Christ the King waits to receive us on the other side.

Right now He is the King and Lord of all history. And He shall be forever. What matters, then, is that we see and acknowledge and respond to Him as Christ the *King*.

The forces around the crucifixion did so by erecting the sign above His thorn-circled head: "This is the King of the Jews." In a way, they were absolutely right in crucifying Jesus, for it was in that very act that He authenticated Himself as our King. He was suffering and dying for us, as the royally appointed Messiah!

Now in our life and in our singing we can proclaim Him as King. As we sing to Him this Sunday, we can live for Him on Monday. Proclaim Christ King, for so He is and will be far beyond the time when this age has seen its day.

Prayer: Our loving God and Father, we thank You for Your guidance and power during all the days of the church year now coming to a close. It has been good to sing of Your love, from Bethlehem to Jerusalem, from the shepherd's field to the mount of Calvary. Help us to realize that our age is moving to a close and that all the world is in Your hands. The song of the angels shall one day silence all the noise of our times, and all the earth shall see that Christ is King. In Your mercy, come quickly, Lord, and grant us peace. Amen.

Prayer before worship: Christ is King and He shall reign forever and ever. Grant us such heavenly vision in this worship hour, Lord, that we see Your Son in His true glory and light. In His name we pray. Amen.

Teaching Us How to Sing

Of all the songs recorded in the Bible, perhaps none has been the subject for more composers' pens than Mary's song. Called "The Magnificat," it moved Johann Sebastian Bach to write one of his greatest choral works.

As we remember the day of Mary, the mother of our Lord, there are few better things we could do than focus our attention on her song: "My soul magnifies the Lord, and my spirit rejoices in God my Savior."

Mary is great because she teaches us how to sing to the Lord. We should sing the best we can, to be sure. Proper breathing is important. Singing on the vowels enriches our tone. Keeping the strict beat makes for the unified song. And the director leading us helps too.

But Mary teaches us other lessons about singing and other requirements for the Lord's song.

She shows us that *joy in the Savior* is what makes for exultant music. She shows us that a grateful and thankful heart will sing the Lord's song best. She shows us that our singing in church must be coupled with a remembrance and concern for those who live in drabness and poverty and have no song in their heart. She shows us that we are joined in our singing by a glorious company of other worshiping singers. Our choir strings from Abraham to Moses to Peter to Luther to saints alive today and all God's children yet to come.

She teaches us to make Jesus Christ the occasion for all our glad songs. We sing, as did she, because the Savior has been promised and even now dwells among us to fill us with good things: forgiveness, peace, hope, love, eternal life.

As we sing, let us always, with Mary, magnify the Lord!

Prayer: Jesus, we can never fully take in the mystery of Your coming to us. Once, in the body of Mary, You were born as a Child, all of Your divinity contained in the Babe of Bethlehem. As your mother received You and worshiped you as Savior, so we praise you as God-made-man. Like her, teach us to exult in the saving work

You did as You suffered and died and rose again to fill us with all good things. Amen.

Prayer before worship: Our Lord and God, we praise You now for men and women of all times and ages who have acknowledged Your Son as Savior and Messiah. We thank You for the accepting faith of Mary, who became the vessel of Your Son's coming among us in the flesh. May He come among us in this worship service through Word and Sacrament that we now share. Amen.

The Word of Truth and Freedom

The festival of the Reformation is a festival of the Word. So was the life and work of Martin Luther. He had a passion for God's Word. He was acquainted with it and saw it as the true treasure of the church.

But Luther knew no word of God outside of a word that cradled and offered Jesus Christ as Lord. The saving, rescuing Christ was the truth for Luther. This saving word of the Lord brought freedom to his heart and soul, so that he could speak and sing and live in joyful service and praise of God.

We shall not celebrate Reformation with profit until we recommit ourselves to the Christ of the cross, revealed in Scripture. Then we will have a living truth to sing of, and we will be free to sing with self-abandoned faith from the depths of our heart.

Prayer: God and Father, we know Your Son as our Savior. Your Word has so livened our faith. We thank You for all reformers in the church who made this blessed truth crystal clear. May we treasure the freedom of our faith now, as we offer songs of gladness to celebrate a living heritage of faith in Jesus Christ. Amen.

Prayer before worship: God our mighty fortress, our refuge and strength, may our worship today turn us back in thanks for all Your faithful reformers of the past and forward to a living confidence that the church is always in Your hands, so that we may sing, "The Lord of hosts is with us, the God of Jacob is our refuge." In Christ's royal name we pray. Amen.

Happy Saints

Of all people in the world, the saints of God are the happiest. And well they might be. Christ has pronounced them blessed, and that amid the most challenging straights of life.

In the Beatitudes of Matthew 5 Jesus says we will be happy when the focus is off of ourselves. So that's what a saint is: one whose attention has been so focused on the needs of the world's people that the self is forgotten—even to the point of being willing to die in martyrdom for the success of the Kingdom.

On All Saints' Day we remember everyone who has died in faith and gone to the Lord. We also urge ourselves to acts of daily dying and sacrifice, so that even now we might taste the blessedness of sacrificial service to the Lord and His church.

O happy saints we are with Christ blessing our efforts now, and moving us toward the great choirs of heaven, where eternal anthems of praise to the Lamb shall be our song forever!

Prayer: Lord Jesus Christ, we come together now, as living saints, to sing of faith and joy in You. Unite our songs with those above, that truly we may be doing the work of heaven here and now. Fulfill this high purpose among us, as You Yourself abide in our midst! Amen.

Prayer before worship: Holy is Your name, Lord God, dwelling with all Your saints above; be pleased to dwell among us in the humbleness of Your Son. Join our hearts and voices now with people of Christ everywhere, so that a joyful noise to Your name will resound in the heavens and on earth. Fill this place with Your glory. Make our worship a foretaste of heaven. In Jesus' name we pray. Amen.

A Grateful Heart

An old prayer for Thanksgiving Day says, "Thou hast given us so much, O Lord. Give us one gift more— a grateful heart!" How true, how true. Perhaps nothing could be more greatly needed by any of us—or so hard to come by!

That seems to be the message of the Thanksgiving Day Gospel. Only *one* of ten returned with a grateful heart to thank the Savior. Not a very good average. And no reason to believe that things are much better among us!

We tend to confine our thanks to days like this holiday, or to church services on Sundays, or to a brief prayer at evening. But Christ would have more than that. He wants a grateful heart, in addition to sentences of thanks at special seasons and times.

This calls for a life and style of living in which we are always returning to give thanks. It calls for a daily life lived in service and sensitivity to others, with humility and grace as leading virtues that shape the thrust of our days.

Knowing what we possess in Christ, and the blessings we have from the Father's hand, we shall have such grateful hearts.

Prayer: God, our privilege now is to offer songs of thanksgiving. Make us equal to the task as we bring to our songs a grateful heart, filled with the love and forgiveness of Christ, overwhelmed by Your mercy and grace. In Jesus' name we pray. Amen.

Prayer before worship: Lord, we are grateful that You have taught us how to give thanks. Your mercies and love are so great that there is nothing else we can do except sing Your praise and magnify Your name. We do it with joy, and ask You to give all worshipers today the same gladness that is in our heart. To the Father, Son, and Holy Spirit be all praise. Amen.